Truth Always Has Its Enemies

The Two Faces of Simon Wiesenthal

Legacy and Testament of Schulim Mandel

Extended and complemented edition 2025

J. A. Mandel

Truth Always Has Its Enemies

The Two Faces of Simon Wiesenthal

A Historical Rehabilitation

This book is the English version of "Die Wahrheit hat immer Feinde", first published in 2019. Translation John Waterfield / BoD.

Bibliografische Information der Deutschen Nationalbibliothek:

Die Deutsche Nationalbibliothek verzeichnet diese Publikation in der Deutschen Nationalbibliografie; detaillierte bibliografische Daten sind im Internet über dnb.de abrufbar.

Verlag:

BoD · Books on Demand GmbH, In de Tarpen 42,

22848 Norderstedt, bod@bod.de

Druck:

Libri Plureos GmbH, Friedensallee 273, 22763 Hamburg

ISBN: 978-3-7528-2005-8

The complete net proceeds of this book
will be donated to the fundraising organization
for Israel **Keren Hayesod**.

KEREN HAJESSOD קרן היסוד
FÜR DIE MENSCHEN ISRAELS

I have based this story on the records and reports of my father (which is to be found in the appendix to this book).

Descriptions of historical places and persons are authentic. The pictures come either from generally accessible sources or from my family album. The dialogues come from my own imagination, because I believe they could have happened in this way.

The renowned Israeli author and journalist Tom Segev wrote a large-scale biography of Simon Wiesenthal, which was published by Keter Books (english version by Schocken Books in 2012). In a paragraph on page 76 he comments on the events this book is based on.

In his book 'Hunting Evil' (Bantam Press, 2009), the British author and historian Guy Walters describes Wiesenthal as 'a liar who made false or exaggerated claims about his academic career and his war years,' so that it would be impossible to make out any kind of coherent picture of Wiesenthal's life in the Second World War.

There have been proven cases where Wiesental subjected victims to further victimisation. My father Schulim Mandel was one of these victims.

J. A. Mandel

Foreword

I have asked many people what they understand by the term 'holocaust'. Their answers were always the same. It has to do with the murder of the Jews and the Nazi concentration camps. Well, you can't say that's wrong! The translation of the Greek word results in the succinct participle 'completely burnt'. And Shoah? That is the Jewish word for holocaust, they told me. Yes, that's right! Actually it comes from the root churban and means 'devastation'.

And then they always went on to say that luckily after the end of the war in 1945, it was all over. But was that really the case?

Among other documents in my possession I have a memoir of my father's, which he entitled his 'Last Will and Testament'. Over many pages he recounts the unspeakable suffering of Jewish families in the last century. From the ghetto to the concentration camp, liberation and... that is not the end of the story. In the life of my father there was the 'Herr Engineer' who, after all the suffering inflicted by the Nazis, after the liberation, added to the burden my family had to bear. This man made himself an indelible reputation as a Nazi-hunter, and yet brought unspeakable suffering on my family.

I have read and reread the manuscripts written in my father's handwriting. For a long time I hesitated. But one day, surely, it will all just have to come to light.

The content of the 'last will and testament' of my father is presented here in the guise of a 'story'. This may not always meet with the reader's approval and consent. But neither does the suffering of my family meet with my approval or consent.

It is already inconceivable, and beneath humanity, when a people – because of ethnic delusions or for other equally incomprehensible reasons – aims at the complete ruin of another people. But cruel and lawless actions of human beings against their own kind, just out of greed or fear, remain quite impossible to fathom.

Will Cain ever cease slaughtering Abel?

Abraham Mandel

Yad Vashem, Hall of Names (Photo: David Shankbone)

Schulim Mandel, passport photo, about 1950.

PART ONE

1939-1945

I
At a distant place in a distant time

Two gentlemen meet. One politely takes off his hat.

'I think we may be somehow acquainted?' says one of them, initiating the conversation.

'Yes, we have met before,' the other agrees. 'It must have been at the end of the war. My memory of it is rather patchy. I was preoccupied with other things at the time, and I had a whole lot going on!'

The other man puts his hat back on and gazes straight ahead as if lost in thought. 'Yes, I can see it as clearly as if it were yesterday. And yet it was such a long time ago. What are you doing now?'

'Oh, I delve around in my jottings. So many names – so many tragedies – so much suffering – so many perpetrators! It would be easy to forget one thing or the other, to get things mixed up.'

'I haven't forgotten anything,' says the man who took off his hat a short time ago. 'How should I address you?' he adds.

'Just call me Herr Certified Engineer. That will do.'

'So you acquired this qualification on completion of your university studies?'

This question being answered in the affirmative, the other goes on: 'But I have information to the contrary. There were a couple of concentration camp prisoners along with you, called Tulek and Tadek. I don't remember their surnames. The fact is that in return for camp privileges you induced them to make false statements in backing up your claim to have acquired a university degree.'

'Well, I suppose it's a case of who you choose to believe. I couldn't show any documents in proof of my degree, as the University of Lemberg had of course been burned to the ground. So I had to depend on witnesses!'

'I have also been told that you found ways of making yourself friends among the German camp overseers. You did this by telling the Germans lots of things that were spoken and planned among the prisoners in secret.'

'Life in the concentration camp was a daily battle for survival,' the man replied, seeking to defend himself against this attack. 'But I was able in this way to make life easier for many of my fellow-inmates.'

'But again only in return for favours. According to my information, plenty of valuable items secretly smuggled into the camp changed hands. Cigarettes for half a loaf of bread. Half a meagre food ration for a medicine. You said you were in twelve different camps. That simply cannot be true. The well-known Israeli historian and journalist Tom Segev unmasked you as having – to put it mildly – exaggerated. He also opined that you were a noisy troublemaker addicted to the limelight, one who always found ways of putting himself in the centre of the picture. He also thought that when the Mauthausen camp was liberated on 5 May 1945, you made yourself useful to the US War Crime Office by supplying them with a list of 91 war criminals.

His interlocutor replies: 'Yes, in the course of my many stints in the camps I may have lost track of some things. But I still thought it important to record the names of those German officers and camp administrators on a list, so that one day they might be brought to justice.'

'And what about the job you were given by the US Office of Strategic Services, to arrest the wanted war criminal Eichmann? Did you really succeed in tracking him down?'

'I don't need to pretend with you, my dear fellow,' comes the answer. 'Of course the suggestion came from me. But the major part was played by the Israeli secret service Mossad, I must admit.'

'And what did the British author Guy Walters have to say about the many inconsistencies in your memoirs? He actually accused you of being a liar about your years of suffering in concentration camps. You always "adjusted" things to your own benefit. Above all with the aid funds of the American Jewish Joint Distribution Committee, for which you were responsible immediately following the liberation. You managed these charitable donations at your own discretion – the author avoids using the word "distributed". Did you hive off money for yourself?'

'You can't say that exactly,' comes the answer. 'I didn't derive any financial benefits for myself. But I did use the funds to set up the institute that later came to be known as the Documentation Centre.'

'And what about the Wiesenthal Fund? On your seventieth birthday the Netherlands even issued a stamp in your honour. Where did the profits go to?'

The question echoes in the void, unanswered. The other has turned away, and vanished in the obscure mists of history.

Commemorative postage stamp of the Austrian Post 2010.

II
Schulim Mandel

The Mandel family comes from the little town of Gródek, not far from Lemberg. As a result of the partition, by 1918 it came under Austrian rule; after that it became Polish, then Russian and today it is part of the Ukraine. What with these political changes, the name of the place has also changed – from Gródek Jagielloński to Horodok.

A visitor to the town will easily recognise that its roots go back to the Austrian royal and imperial house. Many civic buildings with richly decorated façades line the streets and squares. The market place could be an ornament to Vienna or Budapest. You can picture a busy bustle, hasty errands. Kitchen staff, servants or even the lady of the house – as in other parts of the Austrian empire.

Four religious edifices form part of the city centre: the church of the Elevation of the Holy Cross, the church of St John the Baptist, the church of the Annunciation and the church of the Holy Spirit. These houses of divine worship testify to the Catholic faith of the population. And then too there was a still a synagogue. This was the place where 25% of the population – that is how many Jews were living in the town at the start of the past century – were obliged to go in order to practise their faith. Of something like 16,000 people who lived in Gródek in the year 1900, 3610 were of the Mosaic religion.

The town became known as a result of the Battle of Lemberg, where the Austrian royal and imperial Third Army was defeated by the Russian troops under General Nikolai Russki in the autumn of 1914. In connection with this battle the name of Georg Trakl is often cited – an Austrian lyric poet connected with the Expressionists, who served as a military pharmacist and saw hundreds of wounded soldiers die of inadequate care. Trakl processed these traumatic events in his well-known poem 'Grodek'. Not long after, on 3 November 1914, the poet died of an overdose of cocaine.

15

At evening the autumn woods resound
with deadly weapons, the golden levels
and blue lakes, over which the sun
rolls darklier now; the night embraces
dying warriors, the wild cry
of their broken mouths...

(excerpt from the poem 'Grodek' by Georg Trakl)

In 1939 the Mandel family was living in one of those bourgeois mansions on the high street. Beneath the colonnades traders and craftsmen set up their stalls. This too was where the Mandel leather business plied its trade. The German army invaded Poland in a lightning attack. Capitulation followed just over a month later. From then on German government was imposed on the country, and the unspeakable suffering of the Jewish population began.

From one day to the next the German military administration kept issuing new decrees: forbidding Jews to practise professions, imposing lockouts, banning the open practice of the Jewish Orthodox religion and a whole lot more. Finally a construction detachment of the Todt Organisation – a building brigade based on military discipline – came on the scene, to start walling off of what was to become the Jewish ghetto.

Schulim Mandel was just 21 years old when a letter came from the 'Jewish Council' informing the family that they had to move into the ghetto. Schulim came of a Jewish Orthodox family. For one generation they had been engaged in the leather trade, which had earned them a comfortable life in this small town. The sudden change in living conditions hit the Mandels badly. It was not easy for them to give up a stately town house for a diminutive cell in the ghetto.

But Schulim Mandel was a resourceful character. He knew how to make friends among the guards, who to begin with were Poles. As a result he was able to leave the ghetto at times (of course this was strictly forbidden) to procure leather. So they were able to do repairs, as well as making shoes and bags. To the astonishment of the ghetto residents, their customers often included German soldiers. These sent products from the Mandels' leather business back to their families in the Reich, where after two years of war leather goods had become practically unobtainable.

But things soon changed. The ghetto came to be constantly guarded by German soldiers, which made illegal sorties impossible. The Mandel family thus lost its source of income, and what had initially been an almost comfortable life turned into a battle for survival. One day a rumour went around that the ghetto was going to be closed and the inhabitants moved elsewhere. And in the late autumn of 1943 that was what happened.

The drone of the approaching army lorries in the morning twilight was unmistakable. The convoy was accompanied by personnel carriers, each manned by numbers of heavily armed soldiers. Then the sound of the loading flaps being opened shattered the day just dawning, followed by the bellowing of orders from the guards.

The troops charged into the ghetto. Orders to open doors were shouted from many throats within the ghetto walls simultaneously. The ghetto residents were told to pack up their belongings, just the bare minimum. The anxious murmurs of the crowd mingled with the nervous barking of dogs held on the lead by their handlers.

Officers waved lists and called out the names of those who were to be forcibly removed.

In a few hours the ghetto inhabitants found themselves on the army lorries heading for the Warsaw ghetto - for the time being. The ghetto in Warsaw was not the end of their horrible journey. Soon Schulim Mandel was shipped on with his brothers Selig and Jacob.

Their destination this time: the Izbica ghetto.

.

III
Simon Wiesenthal

Nine years before Schulim Mandel, Simon Wiesenthal was born on New Year's Eve 1908 in Buczacz, in Galicia, then part of the old Austrian empire. Today Buczacz is a Ukrainian town with some 12,000 inhabitants. It is situated in the oblast of Ternopil, around 65 km south of the district capital on both banks of the river Strypa.

In this small township with a largely Jewish population, Wiesenthal's father Asher had a sugar wholesale business.

After attending secondary school, Wiesenthal, who was unable to enrol at the University of Lemberg in view of antisemitic restrictions, went on to study architecture at the Technical University of Prague. Having completed his course, in 1932 he returned to Galicia, where he married the love of his youth Cyla in 1936 and opened an architectural firm.

With the Hitler-Stalin pact in 1939, eastern Poland, including Lemberg, became part of Russia. Wiesenthal's licence to practise as an architect was revoked. He had to close down his office, and hire out his services as a simple technician. His future camp comrades Tulek and Tadek will have something to say about this at a later stage. They became Wiesenthal's willing accomplices.

In 1941 Germany launched Operation Barbarossa, its attack on the Soviet Union. As a Jew, Wiesenthal was arrested in Lemberg by members of the Wehrmacht's Nachtigall Battalion, a military organisation of Ukrainian nationalist volunteers. He was accused of belonging to Polish resistance groups, but his wife was able to shield him from the intervention of the deportation authorities.

Lemberg was occupied by German troops on the morning of 30 June 1941. On the very next day, outrages and acts of violence against the Jewish population occurred. Wiesenthal and many other victims were thrown into the municipal prison. It was standard practice by the German invaders to force Jews to carry out the work of cleaning up. Alongside the paramilitary Ukrainian troops, they were obliged to take part in these humiliating rituals, as has been described elsewhere.

Under the command of the German major Josef Salminger some 100,000 souls of Lemberg's Jewish community were subjected to inhuman degradation. The mayor soon found ways of persuading the town's Polish population to do the dirty work of persecuting the Jews. In the ghastly excesses that followed, Wiesenthal was led out onto the market place by a Wehrmacht death squad, to be publicly shot like so many of his fellow unfortunates. The sound of the church bells ringing for midday put an end to the bloody proceedings. One of the officers yelled, 'Stop! Time for lunch.' In the confusion that followed, Wiesenthal was able to mingle with the crowd and so got away from the Germans.

This seeming freedom, however, did not last long. He was seized by Polish secret service operatives and taken to the Gross Rosen concentration camp. Wiesenthal's notes on the horrors in Lemberg not only referred to Major Salminger as a moving spirit of the massacre – the divisional commander Major General Hubert Lanz and the later City Commandant Karl Wintergerst also found a mention. They had the distinction of being the first Nazi criminals whose names Wiesenthal noted. It was the start of a long list, which at the end of the war would become highly significant.

Major Salminger also played an inglorious part in the German surprise attack on the Greek village of Komeno, where the troops under him executed 317 people by firing squad. He himself was later captured and shot by Greek partisans. Major General Hubert Lanz was also responsible for shooting 4000 Italian soldiers who refused to surrender their arms to the German military after Italy opted out of Hitler's war.

City Commandant Lieutenant General Karl Wintergerst played the most sinister role in the Lemberg pogroms. He was captured by the Americans, handed over to the Soviets and since then has been classed as a missing person.

IV
Schulim Mandel

The ghetto of Izbica was intended to be a transitional camp for Jewish transports to Belzek, Sobibor and Majdanek.

At the time Izbica had nearly 3000 inhabitants. It is situated some 44 km southeast of Lublin.

Here the Jews arrived by night. There were already many Jews in Izbica – Jews from Czechoslovakia, and from small towns in the immediate vicinity. Every room in every building was packed with people, everyone sitting on their luggage. Even the streets were full of people, sitting or sleeping on their few worldly goods.

Izbica looked like a station with people waiting for a train.

There was no way in which the town was prepared to accommodate the arrival of foreign Jews. From way back it had been a depressed locality and marked by poverty, the inhabitants being impoverished Jews for the most part. Few of the streets in Izbica were paved, and even today's inhabitants remember the horrific hygienic conditions of that past epoch. Only well-to-do Jews had clean and spacious residences. The houses lacked sanitary facilities – in the entire town there were just two public toilets; otherwise people followed the call of nature either in front of their houses or by the roadside. Only the rich businessman Juda Pomp, who lived on the market place, had his own WC. This was a wonder to the Jews living in Izbica, who could not believe that it was possible for a house to possess its own private toilet.

The ghetto was separated from the town by a simple wooden fence. Here just a few of the deportees could find work. Several hundred young men were deployed to work on river flood defences. Anyone unable to get money by gainful employment or barter would have nothing to eat. Every day as many as thirty persons died of hunger and exhaustion – wizened skeletons draped in rags.

The resourceful Schulim Mandel again took thought of his craftsmanlike skills. He visited the Jewish Council to learn more about the fate they had to expect. One thing was clear: the ghetto was not to be their final destination. The Jewish members of the ghetto administration did not know where they would be sent or when, but in exchange for a small sum of money they supplied Schulim with the names of customers for whom he was then able to carry out repairs. In the course of these activities he also came into contact with cloth suppliers, and so was able to build up an almost professional business in a region occupied and administered by the German Wehrmacht. His life would have been quite rosy, if the occupying powers had not given the Jewish Council the order to assemble a weekly contingent of Jews for deportation. It was no secret that the German-speaking Jews on the Council and the Jewish police favoured Polish Jews for the deportation listings. The social divide within the ghetto could not be overlooked. German-speaking Jews who had formerly been well off contrasted with large families of Polish Orthodox Jews, who had had to scrape out a living in the most miserable circumstances, without money, running water or toilets. Schulim Mandel was not in the former category, but he did not fall in the latter category either. And yet he was put on the list. In the late autumn of 1942 Hitler's army lorries were at the door. With bellowed orders and blows of rifle butts, the Jews whose names were listed were forced onto the loading flaps of the vehicles. Word had been passed around about their destination. It was to be the labour camp in Majdanek.

As the heavy lorries left the town, the remaining ghetto inhabitants were forced to assist in the desecration of the Jewish cemetery, carrying gravestones from the vandalised graves on their backs to the building site where an extension of the local prison was in progress.

V
Simon Wiesenthal

In the time between 1941 and the end of the war in 1945, Wiesenthal was an inmate of various concentration camps, including Gross Rosen, Buchenwald, Plaszow and finally Mauthausen. Mauthausen is a market town in Upper Austria. Situated on the Danube, in 1939 it had around 5000 inhabitants. In the 19th century Mauthausen had been noted for its granite quarry. Among other purposes, stone from here was used to construct prestigious buildings on the Vienna Ring Road.

Mauthausen had been an independent camp as early as 1939. A perimeter wall 2.5 metres in height, and with a length of 1668 metres, secured the facility. The wall was surmounted with a 380 volt electric fence. The entire area of the camp came to around 25,000 square metres. By the end of the war in 1945 something like a million and a half prisoners were held in the camp, forced to perform gruelling labour duties, mainly in the stone quarries. The motto was 'annihilation by work'. One of the particularly cruel features of the place was the 'death stair' – a stone ascent of 186 steps connecting the 'Vienna Ditch' quarry with the camp itself. Here the convicts had to drag heavy granite blocks over a distance of 31 metres to the top. Many of the inmates of the camp failed to survive these tortures.

For the prisoners, the daily routine was always the same: morning call at 4.00 am, make beds, wash, breakfast, morning roll-call at 5.30. At 6.00 the work detachments left the camp, returning at 6.00 pm.

A particularly nasty feature was the evening roll-call, which considerably cut short the supposed 'free time' of the inmates. By the time all the blocks had been counted in the line-up, any counting errors rectified and the numbers updated, as many as three hours could pass – a time during which the convicts, exhausted, undernourished and exposed to the cold in the worst of the winter season, were forced to stand in formation. Lights out was at 9.00 in the evening, after which prisoners were not allowed to leave the barracks. There were three work detachments:
- Internal detachment
- External detachment
- Quarry workers.

Selection and assignment was based on professional qualifications, but also to some extent happened by chance.

Of course assignment to the internal detachment was the most desirable. More by luck than because of the profession he had stated, that of 'technical draughtsman', Wiesenthal was assigned to the central office. Here he was able to document daily proceedings, often horrific, in the everyday life of the camp. It must be said, however, that sometimes his veracity may be doubted. For example, three German soldiers, Wilhelm Schmidt, Günter Billing and Manfred Pernass, were captured as spies behind the enemy lines in the course of the Ardennes offensive, and condemned to death by firing squad. The sentence was carried out at the Mauthausen concentration camp. Wiesenthal was inspired by these events, and illustrated them with a drawing that deviates from the actual circumstances (of death by firing squad). The picture appeared in his book published by IBIS in the first year after the end of the war.

In the late winter months certain changes in the order of the camp made themselves noticeable. Wiesenthal was able to observe a significant reduction in the numbers of uniformed guards. The camp officers who had been responsible for the daily roll call vanished from one day to the next. One day Wiesenthal was on telephone duty. On the other end of the line was the aged commandant of the Vienna fire brigade. What was he to make of this order to second his decimated force as guards for the Mauthausen concentration camp? He only had a few old men and boys. Wiesenthal frowned. He had already learned from the fleeing Nazi guards that the Americans were not far away. Evidently the camp commandant, SS Standartenführer Franz Ziereis, had asked the Vienna fire department to take on the task of guarding the camp, for want of more suitable personnel.

Wiesenthal realised that even if a semblance of discipline was preserved, things were starting to fall apart. On certain days the daily roll call failed to happen, without there being any reason given. And it was the same with breakfast. On the other hand the convicts were surprised that they were suddenly given a more substantial meal at midday and in the evening.

Wiesenthal found out that large quantities of foodstuffs were kept in the stockrooms. As part of the guard force and the administration staff had now left, there was a certain superfluity to be disposed of. All this pointed to the approach of the Americans.

The most welcome development for the convicts still capable of working was the termination of labour in the quarries. This seemed to mark the beginning of a new era of peace and humanity.

These 'non-working days' Wiesenthal spent on the bunk in his barracks, where he had been transferred after an operation on a gangrenous toe. Here he started to compile his list, which would contain the names of 91 Nazi war criminals to begin with.

Born in 1905 in Munich, Franz Ziereis was a German SS Standartenführer and commandant of the Mauthausen concentration camp. In the last days of April he fled to his nearby hunting lodge, where he hoped to hide. However he was discovered there on 3 May 1945, was shot while trying to escape from American soldiers and died on 25 May.

Shortly before this, 'Herr Certified Engineer' (who now had a body weight of just 55 kg) got ready to welcome the 11th Tank Division of the Third American Army under Colonel Richard Seibel. The latter allowed Wiesenthal to assist in the retrospective photographic documentation of the liberation of the camp ordered by General Eisenhower. In one of the pictures, a hastily hoisted transparency from some stock of American props carried the confusing message, 'The Spanish Antifascists Welcome the Liberating Powers'.

VI
Schulim Mandel

From late autumn of 1942 to 23 July 1944, Schulim Mandel was a prisoner in the Majdanek concentration camp, the official name of which was Lublin. Initially it was set up as a 'POW camp of the Lublin Waffen SS', before being redesigned as a death factory.

The camp was located in the Majdan Tatarski suburb of the Polish town of Lublin. The name of this suburb also gave rise to its later name, Majdanek. According to the latest estimates, around 78,000 people, 60,000 of them Jews, were murdered here. Majdanek was both a concentration camp, and also – at least for a temporary period – a death camp.

At the time of Schulim Mandel's internment, a clothes workshop had been set up under SS management, where materials resulting from so-called 'special missions' (shoes and garments from Jews killed in the 'cleansing' process) were sorted, disinfected and patched up. Here Schulim Mandel's skills were in demand. Presumably it was his craft skills, along with his talent for organisation, to which he owed his survival. In the postwar years he learned that he had been working for Deutsche Ausrüstungswerke (DAW) [German Equipment and Supplies], which in 1942 achieved the highest turnover of all comparable Nazi enterprises.

The numbers of camp staff grew as the camp was extended. At the end of 1943, 1258 people worked in camp administration, 261 of them in the staff office. Until the dissolution of the camp, around 78,000 people, among them 60,000 Jews, lost their lives at Majdanek. When the Red Army approached Lublin, the prisoners were driven out on forced marches (later known to history as 'death marches') for transfer to other camps.

Arthur Liebehenschel was the last of five camp commandants and garrison commanders. Having been taken prisoner, he was first interned and then tried at Nuremberg. He was handed over by the United States armed forces to Poland, where at the end of 1947 he was condemned to death, and executed on 24 January 1948.

The death march from Majdanek to an unknown destination went on day and night. In the early hours of the morning when day had not yet dawned,

Schulim Mandel crept to the side of the road during a halt in the march. This break of just a few hours was nothing like enough to give a completely exhausted man the chance to recover. On the contrary, he was obliged to dig holes in the earth to dispose of the bodies of the recently dead. Schulim Mandel spotted a thicket right by the side of the road. As if he wanted to relieve himself, he stepped towards the first tree trunks, which he saw were birches. Later he couldn't really say with certainty, but the black and white

Majdanek Concentration Camp, photo taken by a surveillance aircraft of the Western Allies 1944.

of the trees against the stripes of his convict's uniform may have resulted in the ideal camouflage. At all events he was able to slip into the wood without being noticed. In the early morning it was still quite cold, though it was midsummer. In order to keep warm, Schulim moved on as energetically as he could. He had no idea where he was. As if by miracle, he reached a fork in the road where there was a signpost which he could decipher. A small road led to Legnica, the distance being given as 113 kilometres. When he later thought back on his laborious journey, he had to admit that he had really been very careless. He just strode off without considering the fact that the country was still in German hands, and detachments of soldiers might appear at any time. But nothing of the kind happened. On the contrary, he hit upon a small farming settlement. A cottage gave him the first peaceful night he had had for days. In the morning he was served a generous breakfast by the farmer's wife – bacon, eggs, bread and a jug of tea.

After that he tried on some clothes, and was given a civilian farming outfit. When he gratefully took his leave, one of the farmers gave him a linen bag containing bread and applies. That had to last him until he reached his goal. And he made it! Schulim Mandel reached Legnica on the fourth day of his peregrinations. He had chosen to arrive late in the evening, with a view to checking out the town and finding a place to go. He noticed German soldiers, officers in jeeps, a few tanks, none of them drawn up in an orderly manner as one would have expected of the Wehrmacht. Could the end of the war really be at hand? Schulim Mandel was lucky. Wandering around in the late dusk he happened upon a civilian who addressed him in Polish. When the man realised he was a refugee from the Nazis, he conducted him to a friend's house where he was immediately taken in. Legnica was to be his home for some time.

Legnica (Liegnitz in German) is a city in the voivodeship of Lower Silesia in the southwest of Poland. It is situated on the Mid-Silesian plain at the mouth of the Carna Woda, 60 km west of Breslau. In the year when it was liberated by the Red Army, it had 25,000 inhabitants.

VII
Simon Wiesenthal

Mauthausen, May 1945: it was one of the first days following the liberation of the some 18,000 prisoners of the concentration camp.

Supported by two orderlies, an inmate of the camp dragged himself into the office of the American Colonel Richard Seibel. The colonel would never forget the impression he created. 'A skeleton, with striped pyjamas hanging off him. A man who could still speak with his eyes.' The Holocaust survivor, later to be (by his own declaration) a 'professional witness', Simon Wiesenthal had it put on record that he had 'extracted' from the mouth of Mauthausen commandant Ziereis, then lying on his deathbed, that four million people had been murdered in the camp. The statement is controversial: did it emanate from Ziereis or from Wiesenthal? If the latter had heard the 'confession' of the camp commandant, this would mean that there were three different versions of this scene.

From now on, Wiesenthal assisted at the interviews on a daily basis. He requested to be allowed to work for the US unit responsible for the investigation of suspected war criminals. He was given pencil and paper. Wiesenthal drew up a list of 91 names, with descriptions of the inhuman deeds he remembered having witnessed. For example, there was the SS guard Hujar in the Plaszow camp – winner of many bets, 'because he was able to shoot a bullet through two heads at one shot'. In July of the same year he was commissioned by the OSS (Office of Strategic Services) to search for Eichmann. Together with other victims of persecution and displaced persons, Wiesenthal then proceeded to set up the 'Jewish Central Committee of the US Zone of Upper Austria'. Two years later this gave rise to the 'Centre for Jewish Historical Documentation'. This organisation engaged in the collection of witness statements, at first in the form of a simple questionnaire which was distributed in the camps of displaced persons and filled out by survivors, as well as in the evaluation of evidence pointing in the direction of suspected war criminals, in cooperation with international documentation centres, the police and the judicial authorities. As a result, files and card indexes were created about Nazi criminals and patterns of Nazi crimes.

The documentation centre was housed in a tiny office, was always short of money and was dependent on the work of many unpaid volunteers. Only through small donations and the use of private funds was it possible to keep the operation going.

VIII
Schulim Mandel

Legnica or Liegnitz is the biggest city in the north of the voivodeship. It was heavily destroyed in the war, but some historic buildings remain in the centre. The parish church of St Peter and St Paul on the market place dates from the 14th to 15th century, boasting two very handsome Gothic portals. The late Baroque town hall dates from the mid-18th century. Also worthy of note, in the interior of the market place edifice, are the 'herring booths'. The eight narrow buildings with arcades were once a fish market. Two of them are decorated with beautiful sgraffiti.

Houses on Legnica market square.

In this delightful setting Schulim Mandel made a fresh start with his post-war life. Not far from the former 'fish booths' he set up the Mandel Leather Trading Company. His business met with a good reception from the local population, which now started to increase rapidly. Soon the company had four employees. And so it went as fate would have it. He met a girl who shortly became his wife – Rosa (or Rachel).

Soon after this, however, the peaceful though hardworking life of the young couple suffered an unpleasant interruption, when they learned of antisemitic outrages perpetrated by the people of Kielce. This city of around 200,000 inhabitants is situated 100 km northeast of Cracow. Already in January the Red Army had entered the city and brought the war here to an end.

On 4 July 1946 there were antisemitic demonstrations in front of no. 7 An der Platny in the city centre, which was where the 'Jewish Committee' had its head office. The trigger for this was a rumour about a supposed child kidnapping carried out by Jews, a story that linked in with legends of ritual murder propagated by Christian antisemitism for centuries. An armed militia forced entry to the building. When the residents escaped onto the street, they were attacked by the mob. The net result was that 42 Jews were subjected to brutal abuse and killed by the raging Aryan population, and 80 injured, in some cases seriously.

The young Mandel family took the pogrom as an unmistakeable sign that there was no safe future for them in Poland. And moreover they were a growing family. In 1947 a son, Abraham, was born to them.

Schulim Mandel learned of the existence of an underground organisation which helped Polish Jews to flee the country and settle illegally in Palestine (this was shortly before the foundation of the state of Israel). The organisation was called Aliyah Bet (Bet for the letter B), and it arranged for the illegal transport of Jews seeking to emigrate to Palestine, circumventing the limits set by the British authorities.

After the end of the war a massive wave of illegal refugee movement got under way. Immigration to Palestine met with almost insuperable resistance on the part of the British, who did not surrender their mandate until 1948, resulting in the establishment of the state of Israel.

The Zionist movement had been active for some time, and had started to set up Jewish settlements in Palestine. After the war, although the immediate threat to their lives was no longer present, a great number of the surviving Jewish refugees felt an irresistible urge to leave Europe, where they no longer had family and friends, and their former possessions were now in the hands of aliens. Even a change of location within Europe was not likely to improve the quality of their lives.

The Mandel family hoped to join this exodus, and got in touch with the organisation which made arrangements for illegal emigration. It was not long before they had a schedule worked out. They carefully noted the place of embarkation, date of departure and name of the ship. Following their arrival in Haifa, the organisation would take care of the rest.

After an odyssey lasting several weeks, Schulim Mandel, with his wife Rosa and baby Abraham, arrived in the port of Haifa.

Arrival in the port of Haifa.

It had been clear from the start that the journey was going to end in a kibbutz. The kibbutzim played a crucial part in the settlement of Palestine, and subsequently of Israel.

The kibbutz is a form of settlement, a kind of collective, originally set up in the less developed regions of Palestine. In its beginnings, the everyday life of kibbutz members, or chaverim, was characterised by socialist principles. Each individual provided work for the community without being paid for it. In this new country, Schulim Mandel found it impossible to come to terms with a form of life with which he was unfamiliar. His patriarchal nuclear family was broken up. His son Dziunek was transferred to a children's home, where he now answered to the name of Abraham, and brought up with children of his own age. The parents were given work they were not used to doing, in the central laundry or the tailor's workshop, or even in the fields and stables. Every day the chaverim came together in the communal dining hall, the chadar ochel. This was the crystallisation point of their community life.

It wasn't just the unfamiliar heavy labour – for people who a short while before had been exhausted by flight, and had been exposed to extreme hunger in the camps – that Schulim Mandel and his wife Rosa found testing. His son Abraham was also finding it hard to adapt to the climate of subtropical drought.

One day Schulim Mandel was working in the sweltering heat with a new friend, the two of them endeavouring to make a field into arable land. The friend said to him that he couldn't understand why the English had given this land of Israel to the Jews. Why couldn't they have given the Jews Switzerland? Schulim Mandel didn't find the joke very amusing. The Mandel family stayed no longer than a few months. Schulim Mandel felt obliged, in the interest of the wellbeing of his family, to leave the country now called Israel and head back to Europe. Based on various indications, he resolved to apply for accommodation in a camp for displaced persons at Asten in Upper Austria.

Schulim Mandel, an honest KZ inmate, with his son Abraham in Asten camp, about 1950.

PART TWO

1948-1964

I
Displaced Persons' Camp, Asten

Entrance to the Asten camp near Linz.

After the end of the Second World War, something like eight million people were refugees. They were classified as 'displaced persons' – DPs for short. In Austria they were for the most part concentration camp survivors, forced labourers or foreign workers imported by the Nazis. The Yalta conference, held by the Allies before the end of the war, had come to an agreement about the handling of the refugee problem in the immediate postwar period: displaced persons should be repatriated to their homelands. This worked in the majority of cases. But in Austria there were still half a million refugees remaining, mostly Jewish Holocaust survivors, who had lost their way of life in their former homeland and were afraid of the pogroms that had suddenly started. To begin with they were accommodated in big camps. Initially they were the responsibility of the occupying powers. Then the UNRRA (United Nations Relief and Rehabilitation) took charge of feeding and organising them. But there were other aid organisations as well, like the American Jewish Joint Distribution Committee, that tried as best they could to improve the situation of camp inmates. The Austrian government made support payments to displaced persons until they became capable of supporting themselves.

On his return from Israel, Schulim Mandel arrived as planned in Displaced Persons' Camp 117 in Asten, Upper Austria. Here he was advised to get in touch with the aid resources manager. He learned that it was a Jew, a former inmate of the Mauthausen concentration camp, who exercised this function in Asten. There was no way of getting around him.

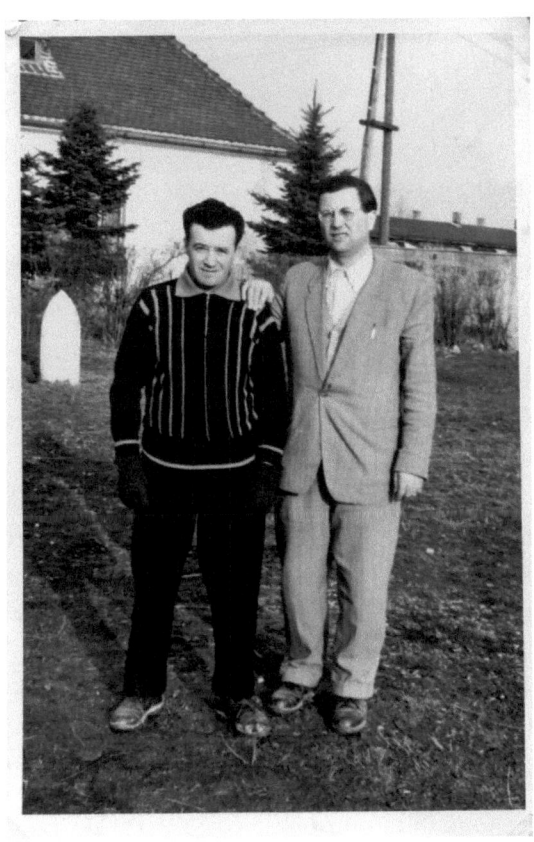

Schulim Mandel with a friend in the Asten camp.

II
First meeting between Mandel and Wiesenthal

Schulim Mandel met Simon Wiesenthal, the coordinator and officer for support payments to former concentration camp inmates, for an interview. The barracks were furnished with every imaginable kind of modern office equipment, coming from American stock. There were rooms for the secretaries, the central card index, interview rooms and the office of Herr Certified Engineer Simon Wiesenthal.

This was the name and title by which he introduced himself, though he mentioned in passing that evidence of his identity and academic credentials had only been furnished on oath by the statements of two fellow concentration camp inmates, called Tulek and Tadek – their surnames he no longer remembered.

At the start of the interview, Simon Wiesenthal talked about the periods he had spent in many German concentration camps. He related miraculous escapes from death by firing squad, from starvation and from having a toe amputated – the toe had become gangrenous as a result of his standing all night rigid on the parade ground in freezing conditions – and mentioned the fact that he had handed a list of 91 German war criminals to the American liberators.

As for his willingness to cooperate with the American authorities, he had been given the responsibility for distributing aid funds from Jewish charitable institutions, as well as the aid payments from the Austrian government. This introduction took up more than an hour. Schulim Mandel could not hide his amazement at Herr Wiesenthal's dealings with fate, and congratulated him on the outcome. Wiesenthal continued: 'From the end of the war till the present day, many Jews have been coming back to Austria. Mostly these have been people who couldn't get on in the countries to which they emigrated, including Israel. Others hope that their presence in Austria may hasten the restitution of their property, not to mention the reparation payments to which they are entitled. It is also a known fact that many refugees are quite simply lured by the prospects of incipient economic growth. I have to say that all this applies to you, Herr Mandel. And that doesn't make your situation any easier!'

Wiesenthal did not wait for an answer but continued:

'Of course you have the possibility of submitting an application to other sources of subsidy. Your status, Herr Mandel, is not without ambiguity. You don't get discharge papers from a concentration camp. And of course you escaped on the occasion of a forced march. Then you tried to establish a footing again in your home town in Poland. But the Polish authorities did not respond to your application for restitution. When you heard of the pogrom in Kielce, you were motivated, quite understandably, to flee the country, and you emigrated to Palestine, illegally it must be said. Leaving the recently founded state of Israel, you then entered Austria once again by way of Italy. Now you have been taken on by Displaced Persons' Camp 117 in Asten. And here of course you can remain, until you are able to support yourself.'

Wiesenthal still had not come to the end of his monologue. 'With an application such as I have described, one that is somewhat complicated in view of the incongruities of the situation, it may be a long time before the process can be completed,' Herr Wiesenthal advised him. He, Simon Wiesenthal, would however have the possibility of intervening, and so cutting short the

Barrack settlement in the Asten camp.

39

tedious procedure of admission to Camp 117 as an inmate with a right to aid payments. For the various favours to the authorities involved in this process, a small charge would have to be made. 'Something like 1000 Austrian schillings might perhaps be sufficient.'

Out of his scanty cash, Schulim Mandel handed over to Herr Wiesenthal the desired sum. After some weeks of waiting, he was told that more was needed. Following a second payment, Schulim Mandel was recognised as a Holocaust victim and registered as a member of the camp in Barrack 39.

Schulim Mandel and his son Abraham in Asten camp, about 1950.

III
Business licence

After a few months of acclimatising to the everyday life of the camp, Schulim Mandel thought of taking up his work in the textiles sector once more. But to do this he needed a licence to trade. This turned out to be a very rocky road. As an applicant, he had no relevant documents whatever to show. What concentration camp prisoner could ever have held onto such things? The responsible government department in Linz advised him to contact the authorities back home in Poland. Schulim Mandel drafted a letter to the municipal council of Legnica, requesting them to send him a copy of his former trading licence in the textiles industry. The application was returned to him around two months later, not having been dealt with. They told him he needed to contact the voivodeship of Lublin. They might still have copies of these documents in their archives. The Central Professional Register in Legnica had gone up in flames in the fighting of the war. So Schulim Mandel drafted another letter. This was answered some months later, to the effect that the applicant would have to provide official confirmation of his identity.

There is a limit to any man's patience. Schulim Mandel was at the end of his.

He asked for a meeting with Herr Engineer Wiesenthal. He did not have to wait long. Wiesenthal received his visitor with elaborate friendliness. They shook hands and enquired about their mutual wellbeing. Schulim Mandel was able to report that his son Abraham, who had been ailing previously, had made a good recovery since returning to Austria. He had speedily put on weight and was now a normally strong little boy. With great delight, he also told the other that his wife was pregnant again.

Simon Wiesenthal's joy was not pretended. He congratulated his visitor, and pronounced the Jewish wish for his future happiness.

Schulim Mandel was touched. He thanked Wiesenthal warmly, and then got down to the business at hand: he had not been able to get hold of his old trading licence from Poland to pass it on to the Austrian authorities. Was there anything that could be done?

Herr Wiesenthal scratched the back of his head in a gesture of indecision.

'Do you realise, Herr Mandel, what bureaucratic hurdles have to be got over, generally speaking, in order to obtain a trading licence? And now in your special circumstances...'

Herr Wiesenthal rummaged in a drawer, got out a form and showed it to his visitor. Schulim Mandel studied the listing of requirements for obtaining a business licence.

MANDATORY DOCUMENTS TO BE SUBMITTED FOR OBTAINING A BUSINESS LICENCE

For individual businesspersons (natural persons) with at least 5 years residence in Austria
- Passport(s) of the applicant(s)
- Residence permit in the case of third state nationals (with the exception of Switzerland)
- Documentary evidence of academic qualifications, where such exist
- Declaration relating to reasons for an exclusion from business in keeping with § 13 of GewO 1994 [Business Code 1994] for natural persons
- In case of a change of name, the marriage certificate or document evidencing the change of name must be additionally supplied
- Where residence abroad or residence in Austria has been less than five years, must be additionally supplied:
    ✻ a certificate from the criminal register of the country of domicile (no older than three months)
    ✻ Birth certificate and evidence of nationality or passport of the applicant(s)
    ✻ Confirmation of registration
- In the case of startup companies, additionally:
    ✻ Confirmation from the responsible Chamber of Commerce in accordance with the Neugründungsförderungsgesetz (NeuFöG) [Act on Subsidies to New Companies].

Schulim Mandel laid the paper aside. He knew that he could not possibly supply the necessary documents. He turned helplessly to the other.

Simon Wiesenthal knew what could be done. He was acquainted with a member of the state government, District Commissioner and Councillor Dr Hofinger. He was the one who held all the threads in his hand, and he, Simon Wiesenthal, would put the case to him. Undoubtedly that would resolve the problem.

What Schulim Mandel had no suspicion of was Wiesenthal's knowledge of Dr Hofinger's past. Any Councillor who had begun by denying that he had ever been a member of the NSDAP would be disclosed to the Austrian illustrated paper Echo as a prominent turncoat. Dr Hofinger had been a Nazi party member (party membership no. 6,371,884) since 1 May 1938. He enlisted in August 1939, and ended his military career on 12 October 1940 in France, where he became sick with dysentery. By the end of the war he held the position of Deputy State Councillor. After the collapse of Hitler's Germany he rose like the phoenix from the ashes, as Secretary in the service of the Deputy State Commissioner Dr Blum. This man was responsible among other things for implementing a programme of political sanitisation, and exercised his office, with Hofinger's help, with great precision.

After just a few weeks, the thing Schulim Mandel had hardly believed possible materialised, when he received a licence to trade, made out by the responsible Linz State Department, for wholesale dealing in textiles and leather and tailoring. But of course this came with a price. Apparently Dr Hofinger had had to draw up various documents and supply certification of their authenticity. This involved stamp fees, submission fees, writing and copying fees, certification fees... Who was getting the fees for what?

At some point it dawned on Schulim Mandel that the fees were going to 'Herr Certified Engineer'.

Schulim Mandel was successful with his business. He was able to inform the authorities that as a result of the income from his company, he no longer needed any government maintenance payments for himself and his family.

IV
The stamp

A rumour went round the camp that an inmate was in possession of a valuable stamp.

This was the time of the first Philatelists' Congress in the postwar years, which took place in Salzburg.

One of Schulim Mandel's customers was the elderly Moshe Frajmann, whom he had known from the old days in Asten. They talked about the past, and Herr Frajmann was unreserved in congratulating Herr Mandel on having got his business back on its feet – and they also glanced at the future.

'You know there's a Philatelists' Congress coming up soon in Salzburg. I hear it's also going to involve a trade fair. This is the first event of its kind in Austria. I mean to go.'

'Are you interested in stamps, then?' asked Schulim Mandel.

'Yes, very much so!' was the customer's reply. If you have a moment, I'll tell you why.'

With growing astonishment Schulim Mandel heard about the valuable Japanese stamp, and how its possessor had managed to save it through the concentration camp years.

Before the Germans invaded Poland, the Frajmann family had a stamp shop in their home town. But the shop's daily business was not the most profitable sector of the company. They made their money by acquiring and selling valuable specimens among collectors. One of the most valuable was a Japanese stamp.

The Nazi invasion of Poland was followed by the deportations, and the Frajmann family wondered where they could hide this valuable stamp, which might one day save lives. They hit upon an unusual, but in the end very effective idea. A number of unremarkable stamps from Japan, together with the valuable Japanese stamp, were stuck on an envelope with a fictitious address. With many folds and blemishes, this was made to look like a valueless used envelope. In this form it survived many personal searches. It was no problem to keep it with you and take it anywhere, and along with its owner it outlasted the Holocaust.

'Today of course I keep the stamp in a safe at the bank,' Herr Frajmann told Schulim Mandel. 'But I've decided to sell it. I'm not as young as I was. I can't eat the stamp, I can't clothe myself in the stamp or live in it. But with what I make from the sale I should have all I need till the end of my days.' Schulim Mandel was reminded of Herr Frajmann's story when he visited Simon Wiesenthal to discuss the monthly dues from the leather business, and the conversation took an unexpected turn. What did Herr Mandel know about a valuable Japanese stamp from the Asten camp? Simon Wiesenthal enquired.

Schulim Mandel told him he was acquainted with the identity of the owner of the valuable stamp. Wiesenthal appeared highly delighted. He thanked him for the information, and stressed that he would be willing to help him out in return at any time. As far Schulim Mandel was concerned, this was the end of the story. He never heard what happened after that. But Wiesenthal's promise to help him if he got into any kind of sticky situation was very reassuring.

And so it turned out. Wiesenthal kept his promise. An announcement was placed, in the Federal Gazette of the Austrian Republic, that any Holocaust survivor who since the war had chosen Austria for his principal abode would be entitled to a certain sum by way of financial restitution. Schulim Mandel could do with the money, as he was just planning to expand his business.

Wiesenthal promised to curtail the bureaucratic formalities, so he could obtain the one-off payment sooner. And by now Schulim Mandl was no longer surprised that he had to pay 'Herr Certified Engineer' a ten percent commission on the sum he expected to obtain – in advance.

V
The case of Pinkas Erdan

Schulim Mandel received a visit from Herr Blum.

Herr Blum had been known to him since the families had been living alongside each other, in the first period of their stay at the Asten camp.

'You still remember me, Herr Mandel?' the visitor enquired. 'We were neighbours once, so to speak. But I expect you'll be wondering about the purpose of my visiting you today.'

'Please just tell me what is on your mind,' Schulim Mandel replied. 'If I can help you, I'll be very happy to do so.'

'Well, the matter is only peripherally connected with me. Actually it involves an acquaintance, well, actually he's more a friend of the family. We were together in Flossenbürg for the final period of our concentration camp ordeal. I was a prisoner in what was a new kind of camp at the time, one dedicated to the pursuit of its own economic targets. As the cheapest labour force available, deprived of any rights, we were to be profitably exploited by the new Deutsche Erd- und Steinwerke (DESt) [German Earth and Stone Works], recently founded for this very purpose. In these camps the regime escalated terror into an absolute, highly perfected and, hitherto unheard-of plenitude of power. With forced labour, hunger, arbitrary decisions and mean tricks of every kind, the annihilation of human beings was first planned and then organised in the form of a factory – and by no means in secret either, seeing that terror is most effective when it is most intimidating.

Consequently the construction of the concentration camp was not hidden from the population. Right from the start, both public authorities and private firms were involved in creating the necessary infrastructure and in the building of the camp itself. Even the supply of provisions for the prisoners and the guards was in many cases contracted out to private firms.

I survived, thanks to another prisoner by the name of Pinkas Erdan. He hinted that it would be a good idea if I were to say I was a mineralogist – that way I would be treated somewhat better by the Nazis. I didn't need to be told twice. Although I hardly remembered anything from my time in secondary school, I had the nerve to state mineralogy as my profession, though I had never practised it.

I was unbelievably lucky. I was seconded to administration, and actually only ever asked to do copying work. You didn't ever get into a technical discussion with the Germans. I guess they were too arrogant to discuss rocks and stones with a Jew. But my friend Pinkas Erdan came to a bad end. He was caught out in some petty peccadilloes, and subjected to a series of 'special treatments'. These involved all imaginable forms of torment, designed finally to lead to the death of the unfortunate victim.

The camp commandant Max Koegel, who had been responsible for the death of hundreds of thousands of camp inmates, gave the order in mid-April of 1945 that all prisoners capable of walking should be marched away. On this death march many Jews lost their lives. After the end of the war the commandant went to ground on a farm, using the identity papers of a former concentration camp prisoner, but he was arrested by the American military in Bavaria in June 1946. Under detention in the Schwabach prison, he hanged himself on 26 June 1946.

Pinkas Erdan was incredibly lucky. He was one of the 1600 prisoners unable to walk who were left in the camp, and liberated by the advancing American army.

And here in Asten we happened to meet up again. I was shocked at the state the poor fellow was in. He was really closer to death than to life. But he recognised me and told me all that happened to him in the past and up to the present.'

Schulim Mandel was shaken. Of course he had known in his own person the terror of being interned in a concentration camp. But whenever he heard a story like this, about one of his fellow victims, it sent shivers down his back.

'And now I come to my request, Herr Mandel,' Herr Blum continued.

'Pinkas Erdan is very sick. He gets a subsidy from the "Joint" to the amount of 600 schillings. He applied to the camp administration. This worked a couple of times. But at some point it must have got to be too much for the Asten administrator. He discontinued medical visits, without any compensation.'

'But that can't be possible,' replied Schulim Mandel. 'You can't just deny a very sick man medical treatment, surely?'

'Yes, that is the crux of the tragic situation,' Herr Blum stated. 'The treatment could be resumed, but only on payment of a fee.'

'So what did the doctor want for the treatment?' asked Schulim Mandel.

'The payment was not for the doctor – the money was to be handed over to Herr Wiesenthal. For Pinkas Erdan, that was just the last straw. In his desperation, he submitted a complaint to the Paris office of the American Jewish Joint Distribution Committee, which was where the subsidies were coming from, after all.'

There was a brief pause, then Herr Blum continued.

'Simon Wiesenthal came to hear of what he had done. He lodged information with the Linz Security Department, accusing Pinkas Erdan of spying activities and describing him as a "Communist agent". In those days the word of "Herr Certified Engineer" counted for a lot. The seriously sick man was arrested, and all his personal documents were confiscated. Without them, Pinkas Erdan could not make any further complaint about Wiesenthal's proceedings. The police investigation however failed to produce results, and the sick man was eventually released.'

On the request of Herr Blum, Schulim Mandel tried to intervene with Simon Wiesenthal. The result of his efforts left him flabbergasted. Pinkas Erdan's monthly pension was reassessed at 300 Austrian schillings. This was an amount you could hardly live on at that time, even if you were just barely able to survive. And to add insult to injury, the sick man was given the privilege of getting his laundry done at the camp laundry for free!

Simon Wiesenthal's actions left Schulim Mandel speechless. How was it possible for a human being to act in such an inhuman way? Now it dawned on him how dangerous this man was, if you were not prepared to be compliant.

Schulim Mandel never dreamed that one day he would share the fate of Pinkas Erdan.

ג'וינט ישראל | JDC
יחד בעשייה חברתית

סטארט-אפ חברתי
בן 102 שנים

Joint Distribution Committee (or 'Joint')

Actually the American Jewish Joint Distribution Committee — it was known as 'the Joint' for short.

The organisation was founded in 1914 as an overseas welfare organisation. From 1933 on it focused on supporting the Jewish population of Germany and the areas occupied by the Germans in eastern and western Europe, by such means as donations for hospitals and orphanages, for foodstuffs, emigration funding and to some extent support of the Jewish armed resistance. After the end of the war the JDC became the most important aid organisation for Jewish survivors. It concerned itself with Jewish Displaced Persons (DPs) in displaced persons' camps in Germany, Austria and other European countries, provided money for food, clothing and professional training, and after the proclamation of the state of Israel in May 1948, organised transport for Jewish immigrants. The organisation is exclusively financed by private donations from American citizens and companies.

VI
The Mairowitsch case

In a meeting with Elias Mairowitsch, Schulim Mandel heard about the tragic story of his marriage.

Hannah Mairowitsch was a very pretty woman in her mid-thirties. In her former homeland she had learned pottery as a trade. With this skill in hand, she hoped to enrol at an art college. But from 1939 on, events intervened. She had met Elias when she was 25, and they married soon after. But their happiness as a couple took a tragic turn when she and her husband were ordered to a ghetto by the German government of Poland.

At the same time measures were being passed, on the orders of one Krüger, whom Himmler had appointed as 'Supreme SS and Police Director for the East', which seriously restricted Jewish freedom of movement, with nightly lockdowns and a ban on moving anywhere outside one's present district.

Another measure which was to grow in importance in connection with the process of 'ghettoisation' was the formation of 'Jewish Councils'. These were created as Jewish organs of self government by order of the German occupying forces, with a view to relaying their political policies and directives to Jewish communities. To begin with they were responsible to the German civil authorities, later they answered to the SS and the police. In practice the tasks most frequently assigned to these Jewish Councils, both before and during the creation of the ghetto, was to assemble detachments for forced labour assignments, to organise the handover of any remaining assets of value among the Jewish population and finally, when it came to the dissolution of the ghettos from 1942 on, to take steps at local level to facilitate the deportation of prisoners to the various death camps.

Ghettoisation, in the sense of the concentration of the Jewish population in certain quarters (sometimes sealed off with walls and checkpoints), ran its course in Poland for the most part from April 1940 to the end of 1941. The three biggest Jewish residential centres or ghettos were the Warsaw ghetto (October 1940, set up in a city district that had been declared a quarantined area by the military government in 1939), the ghetto in Lodz (April 1940) and – after the Germans had incorporated conquered Soviet Galicia as the fifth district in their so-called 'General Government' – the

Armbands from a Jewish ghetto.

ghetto of Lemberg (December 1943).

Hannah Mairowitsch and her husband were taken from the Lodz ghetto to a concentration camp. As a result of fortunate circumstances, she and Elias survived the Holocaust and were able to find each other again after the war. Since the summer of 1945 they had been living together in Asten.

Later on there was speculation as to what it could have been that caused the couple to become estranged. Maybe it was the terrible memories of everyday life in the camp, which neither of them could banish from consciousness; or perhaps it was the fact that they had been apart for almost four years. But it could also have been the resurgent and uninhibited lust for life of the young woman which made her turn to another man.

This man was Simon Wiesenthal. It began with small marks of attention on his part, addressed to the lady. Then she began batting her eyelids at him in a suggestive way, and a gift of some value was delivered to the young woman – who for her part was not averse to a first assignation.

It remained unclear to what extent Cyla Wiesenthal knew about her husband's infidelity.

Hannah's husband at all events was well aware of his wife's doings with 'Herr Engineer'. It was an act of desperation when Elias Mairowitsch applied for a visa to enter Sweden. He said he couldn't handle being separated from his wife. He would do everything he could to bring his wife's relationship with Wiesenthal to an end. Shortly before Christmas the couple arrived in Stockholm. Their life together in Sweden was brief and painful. As Hannah told a girl friend, she couldn't go on living like this. Tragically, she proved this admission true. She left her husband in secret and travelled back to Asten. But there she met with a bitter disappointment. 'Herr Engineer' had lost any interest in continuing the romance. Elias Mairowitsch feared the worst. He travelled back to Austria on the heels of his wife, and she was gone from the camp. They informed him that she was in hospital. That was where he caught up with her, after a suicide attempt.

Clearly Simon Wiesenthal found this affair extremely embarrassing. He had to clean up his act – and he did, in his own way. He enlisted contacts in the Upper Austrian government to issue a warrant for the arrest of Elias Mairowitsch, on grounds of illegal entry. He was promptly deported to Sweden again. His wife disappeared without trace.

VII
The Zimmermann case

'No international conventions valid today on the subject of war crimes, genocide and crimes against humanity are subject to any statutory term of limitation. This is in keeping with the first principles of humanity and justice, seeing that crimes against humanity and against peace have a distinct character – the number of the perpetrators, the degree of brutality exercised and above all the number of victims make these crimes different in kind from all individual criminal acts. So we believe, in harmony with international law, that crimes against humanity must be condemned, all the more so in that both the Federal Republic of Germany and Austria have joined other countries in becoming signatories of the convention outlawing genocide.'

These were the introductory words with which Simon Wiesenthal welcomed a distinguished delegation from America to Linz, having been invited to give this address on the subject of 'Statutory Limitation' by the Jewish World Congress.

Schulim Mandel could not have failed to hear that this lecture on statutory limitation, based on a manuscript by Simon Wiesenthal, had been received with total acclaim. But it actually came from Max Zimmermann, a researcher into historical principles, who had been working on a study entitled 'Forgetting Quickly – the Holocaust was Yesterday'. When Zimmermann heard about Wiesenthal's performance before this illustrious American audience, he called the 'Certified Engineer' to account. This resulted in violent arguments between the two, which terminated in a civil case for the forgery of certificates before the Linz Civil Court Senate.

Simon Wiesenthal was in a tight spot. On the one hand he didn't want to own up to anything, and apologising to the author would be beneath his dignity – but the burden of proof was against him. He needed the support of allies.

So Simon Wiesenthal thought of Schulim Mandel, who still owed him a favour.

'My dear Herr Mandel,' Simon Wiesenthal said, 'you must recall how I helped you out by procuring missing documents from your life before

1939. We Jews, of course, have not only been persecuted, we have also been robbed of our identity. That was your experience, Herr Mandel, and now I have a problem of the same kind. You might be able to do me a favour.'

Schulim Mandel could hardly believe his ears. The distinguished Certified Engineer Wiesenthal was condescending to ask a favour of a small textiles dealer who had only just managed to get back on his feet.

'My situation is by no means easy,' Wiesenthal continued. 'As always, the truth lies somewhere in the middle of two extremes. I discussed the text of the address with Herr Zimmermann, and contributed many ideas of my own. Finally he put the whole thing together, and finalised it in the form of a welcoming speech. I can't deny that, even if I wanted to do so. But that doesn't mean that Zimmermann is in the right. What can I do? You must help me, Herr Mandel, to silence this Zimmermann. I really didn't want to take this step, but I will just have to reveal what he was doing in the concentration camp. You were there too, so you must be aware that Zimmermann was a much feared kapo.'

The kapos, who didn't work themselves – they were just supervisors – had foremen assigned to them. Their relatively privileged position corrupted many of those appointed to this role. Their better rations and exemption from physical labour gave them a chance of staying alive for longer. The SS chose prisoners who were prepared to earn the privileges of their position by acting with exceptional brutality. For example, kapos were frequently chosen from condemned criminals, former SA members condemned to internment, captured Jews (see photo of armband, page 49) or political prisoners. It was a tactical decision on the part of the SS from which group of prisoners kapos would be selected, hence the choice of kapos was often associated with a change in the command structures of the camp. What mattered to the SS was that orders should be passed on and put into effect without scruple and with a minimum of friction.

'You must remember how they set up a new subcamp in the region of Ludwigslust, Herr Mandel,' Wiesenthal continued. 'The new concentration camp was located around 30 km south of Schwerin and a few kilometres north of Ludwigslust. Just some 500 metres away from the site of the later Wöbbelin subcamp, as early as the late summer of 1944 there was a small camp set up consisting of wooden barracks – sometimes it was referred to as the Reiherhorst camp.

In February 1945 a first transport of 700 prisoners from Neuengamme was brought to the Reiherhorst camp. These prisoners were mainly put to the task of completing the larger camp nearby. Kapo Zimmermann was in charge of supervising the work. Many of the prisoners claimed, after having been liberated, that he was a real slave-driver. He tolerated no disobedience, insisted on work being completed even if it meant going on late into the night and was certainly involved in the execution of many inmates. Just think back, I'm sure you will remember.'

Here Wiesenthal ended his lecture on the Wöbbelin concentration camp, and looked at Schulim Mandel expectantly. Schulim Mandel thought hard. Of course it was a long time ago. He had been in a number of concentration camps, and had known many fellow prisoners and kapos. But Zimmermann? Could Herr Wiesenthal perhaps give him any more details about the man? No, he couldn't say that he remembered either the name or the person. He hadn't heard of Max Zimmermann before, he had never come across him in a concentration camp, certainly not in the role of a kapo. He was very sorry, but he couldn't act as a witness for Herr Wiesenthal.

Schulim Mandel would learn by intimate experience that Wiesenthal was not a person to be trifled with. You had to be at his beck and call, and do everything he asked you to do. Having him as an enemy could turn out most unpleasantly. And that indeed was what happened.

VIII
Arrest

By circumspection and a lot of hard work, Schulim Mandel had by this time been able to build up a small textiles business. There was a lot of demand, though money was short and the procurement of materials like fabrics and leather was difficult.

One day two police officers turned up in the office of the business.

'Herr Mandel,' one of the officers said, 'we must ask you to come with us

Barbershop, Asten camp, about 1955.

for a short informal enquiry.'

Schulim Mandel was surprised, but he complied with their request and left the office in their company. He didn't put on a coat or take a hat with him, since they had told him, after all, that it would be just a brief enquiry. When he asked if he needed to bring any documents with him, they answered in the negative. They would just be keeping a record of the interview, they said.

A small van was parked outside his shop. One of the police officers opened the sliding door on the side. Schulim Mandel reeled under a violent shove which forced him inside the vehicle. At the same time one of the two officers handcuffed him from behind with the ease of practice. Then the door was closed and the van immediately moved off.

The trip ended at the police station. First of all he was put in a detention cell. The door opened, and a court officer brought him something to eat. Before the man could leave, Schulim Mandel asked him, 'Can you tell me why I've been brought here and locked up?'

Police car „Grüner Heinrich".

The man was not reluctant to talk. 'I think you're being interrogated in connection with a crime. Whether it's something you yourself are charged with, or they think you can give them information about a third party, I'm not in a position to say.' With that Schulim Mandel had to be content for the moment.

After some time, which seemed like an eternity, they brought him face to face with a police lawyer. Now he learned the reason for his arrest.

'Herr Mandel, you are here and in custody because you are charged with the crime inducement to the abuse of public office,' the official told him.

Schulim Mandel was forcibly reminded of the scene when Simon Wiesenthal had asked a commission for expediting his application for a one-off restitution payment as a former concentration camp inmate.

'At the present time you are under arrest pending investigations. The case is relatively complicated. There are statements and contradictory evidence from different parties. We will need to weigh these in the balance before we are able to form an opinion, based on the letter of the law.'

Such was their cryptic justification of his unexpected 'arrest pending investigations'. For the time being.

For the time being... Two hours later, the talkative guard was again at the door of Schulim Mandel's cell.

'Is it dinner time?' Schulim asked with a smile.

'No, Herr Mandel,' the other answered. 'The Herr Doctor has procured further evidence, in the light of which you are to be interrogated.'

'Is that good or bad?'

'I can't tell you that, Herr Mandel, the other replied. 'I'm just supposed to fetch you to the Herr Doctor.'

Soon after this Schulim Mandel found himself entering the office of Dr Hakenberg, the police lawyer who had conducted the former hearing.

'Please take a seat, Herr Mandel,' were his first words.

Schulim Mandel expected that the official would withdraw the charge, apologise and send him home. But it turned out very differently.

'Herr Mandel, not only are you under suspicion of having committed acts of inducement to the abuse of public office, further crimes have now been laid to your charge. I must first of all bring these to your attention. After that we can talk. But for the moment I'm afraid your arrest pending investigation remains in force.'

'Herr Doctor, I don't understand. It's just been a few hours, and there are suddenly more charges against me? How is that possible? Are you researching my past round the clock, as if I were a wanted criminal or enemy of the state? Please tell me what I am suspected of?'

'Well, that of course is the reason why you are here,' the official replied, consulting his documents. In addition to the presumed crime of inducement to abuse of public office, further matters have now come up of which you are suspected.' The man looked up briefly, and fixed his gaze on the papers spread out in front of him. 'I am now officially notifying of these. Of course you will be given a transcript, which you will be able to study at your leisure while in custody, in order to prepare your defence.

Charge 1: misleading the authorities by making false statements about your nationality, origins and profession.

Charge 2: illegally obtaining a business licence.

Charge 3: making false statements about your name and status as a former concentration camp inmate. In connection with this last, the Republic of Austria has suffered damages through the payment of a restitution sum in the amount of 24,000 Austrian schillings.' As a final charge, Schulim Mandel was obliged to learn that he had supposedly bribed an official of the Linz District Commissioner's department.

Dismayed by the unexpectedly prolonged absence of her husband, that same afternoon Rosa Mandel telephoned the police. She was totally shattered on learning that her husband was in custody. When she asked to have a quick word with him on the telephone, her request was refused.

The following morning Mrs Mandel contacted a lawyer known to the family and urgently requested him to take on the case.

It took him a few days to find out about the charges, but when he had done so, the news he brought her was not good.

'Frau Mandel, your husband is in a precarious situation,' the lawyer began. 'We will have to do all we can to refute the official charges in their entirety, but it certainly isn't something we can do overnight.

The lawyer paused for a moment, and leafed through the pile of papers in front of him. 'We will have to get hold of the relevant applications and official records, request copies of the birth register and register of names from the home town of your husband, and look for and find witnesses to the improper official testimony against him. I think you must be aware, Frau Mandel, how much time and effort this is likely to involve.'

Frau Mandel answered: 'Yes, I hear what you are saying. But I beg you, Herr Doctor, please do anything it takes to bring about the acquittal of my husband. I will talk to him and urge him to be patient. He will understand. And when he knows that you are handling the case, he will recover confidence. It can hardly be easy for him to be taken straight from his shop and thrown into prison – confronted with a string of improper, invented and made-up accusations. Who is it actually who laid information against him?'

'Well, I can't see that from the documents. Officially, of course, it's the authorities who bring the charges. They are obliged to investigate anything like this. Can you perhaps tell me whether your husband has got on the wrong side of anybody, could he perhaps have an enemy?'

Frau Mandel was unable to answer this question. Still, she felt more hopeful and looked forward to her husband's being released in the near future.

But that wasn't how it turned out. The lawyer submitted an application for Schulim Mandel to be released, but initially it met with a refusal. Instead he was officially notified of the imminent transfer of his client from police custody to the prison of the District Court in Enns. For the prisoner this meant more rigorous confinement. While he was under arrest pending investigation he could receive visits from his lawyer at any time; now visiting hours were strictly regulated and controlled by the judicial authorities.

Rosa Mandel too found further obstacles put in her way. It seemed practically impossible to arrange a visit to her husband. She immediately submitted a request for a visit, which received no answer. Then she set off to visit the prison offices in person. There she was informed that she would have to wait for the committing magistrate, who normally showed up at ten in the morning.

And so he did. Her name was called out and she found herself sitting across a desk from a justice official whose head was bent over a bundle of papers. He addressed her as she entered, without looking up.

'Good day, Frau Wiesenthal.' Only now did the official raise his head and look at his visitor. Immediately he realised he had made a mistake, and corrected himself.

'Oh, I am so sorry to have addressed you by the wrong name, Frau Mandel. But these days it is about as difficult to get away from the name Wiesenthal as it is to get an invitation to tea from the President of Austria.' He smiled complacently at his own witticism.

But Frau Mandel was not disposed to be amused. She immediately came to the point of her visit:

'I don't wish to make undue demands on your time, Herr Doctor,' she began, and paused for a moment to see how he would react. His face remained immobile. 'Well, I'm sure you know why I am here. Based on the case as my lawyer and I are aware of it, my husband has been accused of numerous suppositious crimes. For years my husband has been running a textiles business and tailoring workshop here in Upper Austria, he has people working for him, he pays his taxes and voluntarily chose not to accept aid payments for Holocaust victims once his business was able to stand on its own feet. He is in possession of a perfectly good business licence, which he obtained by submitting all the necessary papers. It is not possible to get documents from our former homeland in Poland, because all the municipal files were destroyed by acts of war. Nor do we have any discharge papers from the concentration camp issued by the Allies, because my husband managed to escape from one of those "death marches". But the authorities know all this already. So why do you suddenly come up with these groundless accusations?'

'My dear Frau Mandel, the mills of justice grind slowly,' the official replied unctuously, and proceeded to explain to her the due process of law in minute detail.

Rosa Mandel interrupted him in full flow, saying she just wanted a special concession for a visit. The official seemed sympathetic, and filled out a form for her. He got to his feet and handed it over laboriously.

'We are not inhuman. It makes me sorry for you that I cannot reverse either the charge against your husband or his arrest. But the case is too serious for that, and in any case I would not be authorised to do so.'

With these words he showed Rosa Mandl to the door, opened it for her and took his leave with a little bow.

Rosa Mandel hastened along the corridors and finally found her way to the prison sector. There she was shown into an interview room, which was divided in half by a wire netting. She sat down next to a guard, who, she supposed, was obliged to be there to witness her conversation with her husband.

Schulim Mandel entered from the opposite side. He was in handcuffs, which another officer now removed. He looked completely distraught, and Rosa Mandel could see in his face the signs of the privations to which he had been subjected.

Schulim Mandel urged his wife to visit Wiesenthal and ask him to intervene in the proceedings. He was an influential man, and connected with a great number of important people – it would be an easy matter for him to lend a hand and bring about a positive outcome, especially as the accusations were completely unfounded. But it could be a long time before he, Schulim Mandel, could get together the proof of his innocence that was needed, and conditions in prison were anything but a picnic.

Of course she would do this for her husband, and take their son, Abraham, with her. But she cut him off short at this point, as she was aware their time was limited. On leaving the room she cast a last look back at Schulim Mandel, and saw the officer handcuffing him again. Like a capital offender, was what crossed her mind.

IX
Appointement with the "Herr Engineer"

To her great surprise, she was able to arrange an appointment with the 'Herr Engineer' almost immediately.

The meeting with Simon Wiesenthal, accompanied by her sons, was something Rosa Mandel would never forget as long as she lived. At the appointed time she found herself in the anteroom of the office of the Head of the Centre for Jewish Historical Documentation.

To begin with he received her with every mark of friendliness. Simon Wiesenthal chatted about his present and future work. Since 1953 he had been an Austrian citizen, naturalised by the order of the State Government of Upper Austria, as he told her with a certain pride. Now he had just arranged for the dispatch of all the documents he had collected about the Holocaust and its victims to Yad Vashem. 'Over a ton of Jewish contemporary history,' he said. He intended to accompany the shipment himself and spend some time in Israel.

Then they got onto the subject of Schulim Mandel's imprisonment. Rosa could not believe her ears when this man said to her:

'Well, we've had to bury your husband. I'm afraid there was nothing we could to. He should have considered before whose side he wanted to be on. But no doubt he will be resurrected, I mean released, in five years' time. That's just the way it is at present, and even I can't do anything about it. The time will pass very quickly.'

What the Nazis failed to accomplish was brought to completion by Simon Wiesenthal.

X
Aguda Israel

According to the beliefs of the Israeli political party Aguda Yisra'el, national salvation is not to be achieved by the Zionist movement, but only by following all the religious commandments set down in the Torah (the mitzvot). Notwithstanding the party tries to exercise as much influence as possible on the outlook and policies of the state of Israel. This arch-conservative party is supported donations from powerful individuals and financial institutes. Its not inconsiderable funds have long been invested in rock-solid real estate.

Friends suggested to Frau Mandel that she should get in touch with the president of the Aguda Israel branch that had been set up in Austria, Benjamin Schreiber. Perhaps he would be able to help. Herr President Schreiber turned out to be exceedingly helpful. He mentioned to Frau Mandel that he himself had been a concentration camp prisoner, and had been subjected to frequent torture by the kapos. He promised immediately to put at her disposal a house owned by his organisation, both for her personal use and as a kind of assurance or guarantee of her husband's ultimate release.

Everything seemed to be taking a turn for the better, but now Simon Wiesenthal again put a spanner in the works.

When he heard of the guarantee given to Rosa, he pulled out all the stops to ensure that Schulim Mandel's arrest remained in force. Of course he didn't want to be on the losing side.

What happened next beggars belief. The following article was published on December 18, 1950 by the JTA, the Jewish Telegraphic Agency, a press agency founded in 1917 and based in New York City since 1922:

Attempts to establish the identity of the anonymous person who had posted the article proved fruitless. 'Intervention in an ongoing case', as it was termed in official judicial parlance. But for insiders, the Wiesenthal signature was all too plain to read.

This incident held up Benjamin Schreiber's efforts. At the same time, Frau Mandel learned that no visits to her husband in prison would be allowed, in view of a suspicion of conspiracy to escape and the risk of collusion.

Rosa Mandel pointed out the very poor physical state of her husband as a result of his long imprisonment, and asked for him to be given intensive medical treatment. Her request that he be visited by a medical professional and allowed essential medicines was however turned down.

When Simon Wiesenthal heard that individual Jewish fellow citizens in the Asten camp were trying to help the Mandel family, giving them advice, or even speaking to Rosa Mandel, the powerful engineer made sure that the American Joint support funds paid to these people were been withheld. No one was even allowed to speak to the Mandel family! The pressure, especially on Rosa Mandel, grew immeasurably.

Without a single contact person in the camp, she soon lost all hope. In her desperation, Rosa Mandel decided one day to wait for the pastor from Asten in front of her barracks. Always at the same time, the Catholic village priest walked from the village through the camp to the school barracks, where he taught religion to the Catholic children.

When the pastor, a big, fat man with an open face, noticed the crying woman in front of her barrack that day, he spoke to her and asked what had happened that made her so desperate. In tears, Rosa Mandel told of what had occurred to the family and how her husband had been imprisoned, completely innocent. The pastor was utterly beside himself when he had heard everything. His reply, speaking more to himself, was:
"How is it possible that something like this can take place among the brothers of Moses!?"

XI
Release

But at last a turning point was reached in the fortunes of Schulim Mandel. The court finally acknowledged the arguments for the defence, which were submitted in the form of a deposition by Aguda Israel, and set him at liberty.

It was Herr President Schreiber who deserved the credit for obtaining the exculpatory documents in the 'Mandel case'. Whenever it would have been nearly impossible, or would have taken an inordinate amount of time, to get the necessary written evidence, certificates or witness statements, the authority of the Herr President had lent wings to the proceedings.

As a result Schulim Mandel was able to show the authorities all the documentary evidence they needed for proof of his innocence. On the advice of his lawyers, he submitted to the courts a request for indemnification on grounds of unlawful imprisonment, and remuneration of the costs involved in procuring the documents for the defence. The negative response coincided with the court's demand that he pay the court costs and cost of the proceedings as well as personal indemnification.

So Schulim Mandel was a free man, but he had not yet been rehabilitated. Alongside his business activities, he dedicated a great part of his time to the restoration of his reputation.

The Mandel family was now given a demonstration of what could be achieved with the help of an energetic and determined friend. Herr President Schreiber changed lawyer. The new lawyer immediately demanded to be given access to the case files. Where had these charges come from, what documents had been advanced as proof of Schulim Mandel's supposed manipulations? What were the compelling reasons for the incarceration of a man who had no kind of possibility of escape?

The authorities responded sluggishly to the lawyer's request. But once again an order emanating from the District Commissioner had a part to play. In the course of a meeting at the court offices, Schulim Mandel was able to see out of the corner of his eye, the signature of Dr Hofinger on a document lying on the desk.

The applicant sitting opposite the police lawyer by this time knew rather more about the career of this political turncoat, who by contracting dysentery had been transferred from the German army to the risk-free post of a Deputy State Councillor. Presumably his low Nazi party membership number had had something to do with it. Schulim Mandel presented his case, conscientiously and with justice on his side. In the interest of his civic rehabilitation, he urged, he must be allowed to inspect the files of the charges that had been levelled against him.

The lawyer facing him scratched his head – a gesture of indecision. Well, yes… he was sorry, but he couldn't pursue the matter any further. As he uttered these words, he looked sideways at the document on the desk with Dr Hofinger's signature. I'm afraid it is impossible to locate the files, he went on, regretfully. And in any case, the various proceedings involved had come to nothing. Herr Engineer Wiesenthal had seen to that a good while ago.

Schulim Mandel was able to observe how the official bit his tongue. He realised he had said too much.

The Mandel family's lawyer eventually discovered that at this time it was standard court procedure, when files for the prosecution could not be supplemented by further evidence and it was highly doubtful whether they could lead to a positive verdict, simply to make them disappear.

When Schulim Mandel left the courthouse he had not yet succeeded in restoring his reputation. But at least he was a free man.

XII
Bar mitzvah

The bar mitzvah is the ceremony that marks the beginning of religious adulthood for a young man who has completed his thirteenth year. It is based on a legal ruling stating the time from which a young man becomes responsible for observation of the Jewish religious commandments.

Bar mizwa ceremony in Jerusalem.

The bar mitzvah ceremony varies widely in the different progressive synagogues. Generally speaking the candidate reads, on a sabbath morning, the weekly section of the roll of the Torah (some read, some sing, other read and translate), and speaks the set formulae in the praise of God before and after the reading. Usually the young man is responsible for the entire Torah reading, not just the last few verses (maftir) as is standard practice in many Orthodox synagogues.

Friends and relatives present gifts for the young man. They are encouraged to give presents with a Jewish significance, in keeping with the occasion –

some Jewish ritual object, for example. Many families follow the ceremony with a private party to which guests from the circle of family and friends are invited. To the delight of all, the young man is bombarded with sweets, like confetti – which are picked up with enthusiasm and eaten by the children present at the ceremony.

So Schulim Mandel was understandably very disappointed when the party he had carefully prepared, which he had been happily looking forward to, failed to take place. What had happened? Even while his son Abraham was still undergoing religious instruction for the event, a long list of guests had been drawn up and the kosher patisseries ordered. But then one invitation after another was declined. In the end only a handful of guests remained. Yet again, the Herr Engineer was responsible. Either directly or by means of intermediate agents, he let it be known that attendance at the bar mitzvah party for Schulim Mandel's son Abraham could have implications, possibly affecting the ongoing financial support on which the guests (for the most part former camp inmates or refugees) relied.
The bar mitzvah celebration for Abraham Mandel was never made up for!

XIII
The jeans offensive

Schulim Mandel had learned that a large quantity of jeans – at the time they were very much on trend, but not easy to come by and not cheap – was stored at the Vienna customs depot.

When on a visit to the capital he made his move. Paying in cash, he acquired a small number of the garments. These were then offered to the public, in the regular course of business, over the next few days by the Mandel textiles company.

Later on Schulim Mandel was unable to say how information about this perfectly legal transaction could have reached the ears of Simon Wiesenthal. Evidently the man had eyes everywhere, with a finger in every pie.

Completely out of the blue, a legal summons for customs violations and financial derelictions dropped through the door of the textiles firm. Schulim Mandel was charged with having obtained 5000 pairs of jeans, without accounting for them and without regard to import restrictions, and having already put them on the market.

It started the same way it had done before. Schulim Mandel was asked to visit the police station for a minuted hearing. At the door of his shop he looked round the courtyard, expecting to see a small green police van. But no, the coast was clear. Of course the times had changed, and kidnapping was no longer acceptable practice on the part of the executive.

Schulim Mandel reached for the telephone. After he had been put through to a number of extensions, he succeeded in reaching the official who was responsible for his case. He asked him just to conduct an immediate inspection of the Mandel textiles company. That way he could get an idea of the volume of trade and of the accounts. Then they could talk about the case man to man.

Whatever the official may have thought of Schulim Mandel's last words, he turned up on the following day as agreed.

After inspecting the accounts, the visitor took a look at the warehouse. The entire business premises – warehouse, tailoring shop and office – measured no more than 90 square metres, Schulim Mandel pointed out. How could he possibly be storing 5000 pairs of jeans, along with all the packaging?

Notwithstanding, the official said, he was obliged to follow up every indication conscientiously.

At this, Schulim Mandel finally lost his composure. He showed the visitor to a small door. With a polite gesture, he urged him to open it. It was the WC.

XIV
Exodus from Upper Austria

The matter was not followed up further. In the end the official turned out to be understanding, and even friendly. On Schulim Mandel's last visit to the police station, the lawyer pointed to a considerable pile of papers on his desk.

'And every file has your name on it,' he was told. He must have very dangerous enemies in high places, he further learned. And then came a suggestion that was to have consequences – 'Why didn't Herr Mandel just turn his back on the state of Upper Austria and start a new life in Vienna, where it isn't the case that everybody knows everybody.'

XV
Vienna

That year the summer started very early. The sun shone from a blue sky, and people were delighted with the unexpectedly early splendour of blossoming flowers. The Mandel family moved to Vienna. The company made a fresh start in Vienna's second district. Schulim Mandel once again showed his energy and determination.

Once, Schulim Mandel was in the store of a friend's company, Lekotex, on business. The firm belonged to the Weinblatt family and was managed by Franek Weinblatt, who, like Schulim Mandel, originated from Poland. When the two business partners and friends were deep in conversation in the shop at Salzgriess in downtown Vienna, Jidl Frenkl suddenly entered the business premises. Everyone in Vienna's Jewish community knew that Frenkl was a Kapo in the concentration camp, so no one wanted anything to do with Frenkl, who ran a jewelry store in the first district. And everyone also knew that Frenkl was friends with Wiesenthal.

Franek Weinblatt introduced Frenkl to his friend Schulim Mandel, who had never met Frenkl in person before. "May I introduce, this is Mr. Mandel." Frenkl, who was standing by the front door, replied: "Aren't you Mr. Mandel, who has problems with engineer Wiesenthal? You must have committed quite a few crimes. You're not a good guy, it's not for nothing that they locked you up!"

For a moment Shulim Mandel was speechless at this outrageous accusation from a man he did not know and had never met before. After a short pause, Shulim Mandel calmly and composedly replied: "Who are you to allow yourself to make such accusations? Aren't you the infamous Jidl Frenkl, the Kapo?"

Having heard Schulim's reply, Frenkl turned on his heel and left the shop stammering: "Excuse me, ... I must have been very badly informed."

Life in Vienna continued, the conflict between Simon Wiesenthal and Schulim Mandel and the innocent imprisonment in Upper Austria were covered with a cloak of silence by the authorities and by the Jewish Community of Vienna, too. Never was there an apology from the Upper Austrian judiciary for Schulim Mandel's legally unfounded arrest and long pre-trial detention - let alone compensation. It would later turn out that the court's relevant documents on this case had apparently been destroyed at the behest of high authorities in the 1960s, shortly after the events.

Likewise, Wiesental's outrageous accusation and his vicious and unacceptable actions against one of his fellow believers and - as a former concentration camp prisoner - comrade in fate were a taboo subject for the Jewish Community of Vienna. When the renowned Israeli author and journalist Tom Segev was researching his major biography of Wiesenthal, published in 2010, he got insight into Schulim Mandel's legacy through Eli Rosenbaum, the former director of the Office of Special Investigations in the US Department of Justice. Rosenbaum came across the document in the archives of the IKG Vienna. In this legacy, comprising six tightly typewritten pages, Wiesenthal's deceptions and slanders are described in detail. Thus the Jewish community of Vienna was also aware of this fact, but preferred to keep quiet about it.

Nevertheless trade began to flourish due to Schulim Mandel's business acumen, the firm achieved recognition in professional circles. Schulim's son Abraham joined the company, and was being prepared to take it over.

But his father's health was poor. Schulim's years in the concentration camp, the painful trip to the Middle East and return to Europe had left serious marks on him. Massive inroads on his health were also the result of his constant worries, and finally his imprisonment – for all of which Simon Wiesenthal was responsible.

Schulim Mandel was in the habit of saying: 'I got the better of him, but

I didn't carry off the victory.' In the end, this unfortunate man lost the most important thing of all – **his life**.

He died at the early age of 47. Some day, will there be justice in the world?

~

Letter to my father

Papa

I thank the readers of this book for taking interest in your fate. I have endeavoured to capture its tragic aspect – the gratuitous falling out with Simon Wiesenthal which ended by destroying your life – in the form of a historical narrative. The above description of the circumstances was difficult enough. But to find adequate words for the pain – the destruction of one person's life by another, out of low motives – is practically impossible. All the more would I wish that you not only be remembered, but remembered in the light of justice. I want you to know that I have done all I could to pass on your picture untarnished to a posterity where hopefully justice will prevail.

History is like sand in the desert. We human beings, as we pass, leave on it the traces of our lives. The wind of forgetfulness blows over it, carries the grains of sand over the ground, covers the traces and finally obliterates them completely.

I wish your traces may remain clear – that the wind and the sand spare them for as long as possible.

Your son

Epilogue

Although the events described in the book took place more than six decades ago, they do not let me rest. They haunt me during the day and haunt me in my sleep. It keeps coming back. I regularly wake up in the night sweating, roused from my sleep by the injustice done to my family. The unpunished injustice and the vile denunciation by Simon Wiesenthal, which my father had to endure, bothers me more today than it did a few decades ago, when the immaturity of youth protected me from the consequences of the events, at least to a certain extent.

Schulim Mandel spent two months in prison in Enns and Steyr – innocent, based on Simon Wiesenthal's fictitious allegations. My father's state of health deteriorated sharply during his imprisonment, particularly because he was denied his medication. In addition, the man who was already suffering from a weak constitution was denied adequate medical care. Nevertheless the judiciary of Austria or the state of Upper Austria never officially took responsibility for the illness my father suffered wrongly acccused, not to mention rehabilitation or a compensation for the unjustified imprisonment. There was no response whatsoever from any of the officials of the Republic I spoke to. To the Austrian democracy, free opinion is just a beautiful ideal that only exists on paper.

I was in Enns several times myself and tried to do some research at the court and to get access to the case files. However, the district court in Enns has been merged with the regional court in Linz for some time. The files and court records from Enns from the time of Schulim Mandel's arrest are no longer available. "I'm sorry. You know how it was back then," a very dedicated young judge told me. "The judges came to an agreement among themselves and the files were then burned in large barrels. Anything they didn't like was destroyed." Then the young judge added the characteristic sentence: "Back then everything was filled by Nazis".

Is it a coincidence that the files from the cases in which Simon Wiesental was involved disappeared without a trace and no longer exist today?

This means that rehabilitation is no longer possible because the Schulim Mandel case officially never took place. Nevertheless, my father Schulim Mandel died at the age of only 47, also as a result of this imprisonment. The state of Austria thus bears a not inconsiderable complicity in the misfortune that befell my family.

When I was with my mother at Simon Wiesenthal's office in Linz, Wiesenthal said very calmly and completely emotionless: "Schulim Mandel will be released on a very high bail or he will be in prison for five years." It was already agreed upon and that's exactly what it said later in the court record. Even then, in the office of the "Center for Jewish Historical Documentation" at Goethestrasse 63 in Linz, at the age of 12, I realized: Simon Wiesenthal was an ice-cold person, without a conscience and without any compassion for his fellow human beings. I spoke to many people about the conflict between my father Schulim Mandel and Simon Wiesenthal. In doing so, I noticed that the monstrosities that Simon Wiesenthal was capable of, his dark side, are well known to many people. In a conversation with Dr. Leon Zelman, for example, the co-founder of the Jewish Welcome Service Vienna, Dr. Zelman spoke with great credibility about how he had seen Wiesenthal in the concentration camp as a kapo beating up concentration camp inmates. Likewise, the downsides of Wiesenthal are brought up in the major biography by the renowned Israeli author and historian Tom Segev.

Guy Walters dedicates an entire chapter of his monumental work "Hunting Evil" to the person of Wiesenthal. In his 2009 first published book about the efforts to bring escaped Nazi war criminals to justice, Walters meticulously proves that Wiesenthal lied several times about his own role in the hunt for prominent Nazi war criminals. His formulation on page 117 of "Hunting Evil" is unambiguous: "He was a liar, and a bad one at that." Walters goes even further by saying that anyone who had professional dealings with Wiesenthal had to recognize that the man was little more than a showman performing the role of a Nazi hunter. Ultimately, Walters concludes that Wiesenthal's low esteme for the truth makes it possible to doubt everything Wiesenthal ever wrote or said.

Walters also draws attention to Wiesenthal's incoherent, contradictory and sometimes demonstrably false accounts of his whereabouts in 1943 and 1944. Wiesenthal's at least four completely different reports on his activities between October 1943 and mid-1944 raise serious questions, Walters emphasizes. The violent conflict between Simon Wiesenthal and the former Austrian Chancellor Bruno Kreisky, who repeatedly accused Wiesenthal of collaborating with the Gestapo, is also discussed in Walter's book. Kreisky's accusations were based on unfounded evidence from the communist Polish secret service and the dispute, as is well known, ended with Kreisky's defeat in court. However, according to Walters in "Hunting Evil", the multitude of contradictory stories about Wiesenthal's biography from 1943 and 1944 requires that such questions be raised by unbiased researchers.

Wiesenthal's exchange with the OSI, the "Office of Special Investigations", also does not shed a good light on the veracity of the "Nazi hunter" and his contribution to the arrest of war criminals. The agency, which is part of the United States Department of Justice, was from 1979 responsible for prosecuting Nazi war criminals who immigrated to the United States before it was transformed into the Human Rights and Special Prosecutions Section (HRSP) in 2010. Eli M. Rosenbaum, OSI director from 1995 to 2010 and honored with the prestigious Elie Wiesel Award in 2021, finds harsh words for Wiesenthal's methods and accuses him of making Keystone Cops mistakes amongst others in the Mengele and Eichmann cases and, even more, of inexcusably accusing innocent people.

The Jewish Community of Vienna IKG also knew about Wiesenthal's inexcusable accusations and maneuvers and the conflict between him and my father. Schulim Mandel sent his legacy (see page 84) also to the Jewish Community of Vienna, which then apparently felt compelled to demand a statement from Wiesenthal in this matter. Schulim Mandel's legacy and Wiesenthal's harsh reply are in the archives of the IKG in Vienna and are cited as sources by both Tom Segev in his Wiesenthal biography and Guy Walters in his book "Hunting Evil". Although

Wiesenthal's outrageous machinations were already known to the Jewish Community of Vienna and its then president Emil Maurer at the beginning of the 1960s, the IKG remained inactive and preferred to keep the matter under wraps.

When I spoke to Ariel Muzikant, who was president of the IKG from 1998 to 2012, about the incident and my plans for this book in 2015, Muzikant told me bluntly that it would not end well for me if I published anything negative about the Jewish Community of Vienna in my book. It is no coincidence that Muzikant had worked as Wiesenthal's assistant in his Vienna office a few years earlier - he seems to have adopted Wiesenthal's condescending tone one-to-one.

It always looks different from the outside. It is also about the cohesion of our Jewish people. Unfortunately, this cohesion does not stand up to reality, the Jewish people are no different from other peoples. We too make mistakes, there are good and bad among the Jews.

As a child, I witnessed the terrible injustice inflicted on my father by Simon Wiesenthal. The terrible pain that the Mandel family suffered in the Shoah, like almost all Jewish families in Europe, happened before I was born.

Nevertheless, these events haunt me to this day - a fate that I certainly share with the majority of European Jews of the first generation after the Shoah. Both of my parents survived the concentration camp. My father's two brothers and his parents, my grandparents, were not so lucky, they were murdered in one of the many concentration camps in Poland, my mother's family suffered the same terrible fate. Nothing remains of the history of the Mandel family in the shtetl of Gródek Jagiellonski, where my grandfather Abraham Mandel ran a flourishing rawhide trade, everything has been destroyed. All my attempts to find files or records with the relevant authorities in Poland and Ukraine have come to nothing. The only written documents that exist of the Mandel family from before the Second World War are two entries at Yad Vashem in Jerusalem made

in 1947 by Barukh Salamander, a neighbor from Gródek, and containing the names of my grandparents Sara and Abraham Mandel. About
other relatives, such as my father's two brothers Selig and Jacob, or his
cousin Schaja Gerber, who is mentioned in the legacy, his wife Golda
and their children, who, together with other Jews, were doused with petrol by German soldiers in a magazine in Gródek and by were burned
alive, there is not even a Page of Testimony at Yad Vashem - their existence was completely erased by the Nazis.

This terrible blank space in my family history, as well as the injustice
my father suffered, still haunts me to this day. Although these events
happened many years ago, they are never over. Truth is just a word -
whoever has the power determines the truth.

Simon Wiesenthal destroyed my father's life and my childhood. There
will be no justice. An apology or an official rehabilitation for my father
Schulim Mandel maybe - and eventually a normal life.

Legacy of Schulim Mandel

„An meine Söhne ..."

(written 1960)

Schulim Mandel

To my sons Abraham and Fimek, given in Vienna in the year 1960.

In 1953 or 1954 I was summoned to Barrack 40 in the Asten camp to see Ing. Wiesenthal, who I did not know at the time. He explained that he could use the Uro to get me compensation for the concentration camp imprisonment I had suffered. He asked for documents for my concentration camp imprisonment, which I handed him over. Through this I became better acquainted with him. In 1951 I lived in camp 1001 in Wels. At that time there lived a man in Wels I knew only very little. I knew that he owned a Japanese postage stamp that he wanted to sell. He asked me if I could name someone interested in this. I told other Jews about this stamp in the Asten camp. They reported this to Mr. Ing. Wiesenthal, and one day the latter called me to barrack 40. There he had a law office as director of the A.J.D.C. (Joint). He asked me to drive with him in his car to the owner of the stamp and mediate the purchase. He also wanted to reward me for it. I declined a reward but went with him and then didn't care if the sale went through. This is how Ing. Wiesenthal and I got to know each other better. In 1956, Ing. Wiesenthal had me come to his office in Linz. There he informed me that my request for compensation would take a long time, but that he was well connected and could expedite the matter if I agreed to give him 10% of the expected sum. Since I urgently needed money at the time, I accepted his suggestion and the money was subsequently transferred. Back then he was my best friend. Through insights into his behavior and his behavior towards other Jews, I got the impression that he cannot be a good person, but an egotist who is only concerned with his own advantage. The case of Pinkas Erdan made this clear to me: Pinkas Erdan was a seriously ill person who received ATS 600 a month from Joint. One day he fell out of favor with Wiesenthal. Although Pinkas was a seriously ill person, he had his monthly support stopped. Pinkas wrote to the Joint in Paris. Ing. Wiesenthal's answer to this letter was a complaint to the security authorities in Linz, according to which Pinkas was an agent from the East who lived under a false name. Pinkas was arrested and his papers were taken from him. When he was released a few hours later, he was without documents. With this trick Ing. Wiesental wanted to prevent Pinkas, who felt helpless without papers, from being able to complain about him in Salzburg. I learned all this from Pinkas himself, who in 1958 was in the hospital in Linz on the infection ward. At the time, Pinkas had a Hungarian refugee named Hausner tell me that he wanted to eat kosher. I brought the food that Hausner had prepared for him to the hospital in Linz. Pinkas was very depressed and cried a lot and asked me to go to Mr. Wiesental and ask him to send him some support again. I went to Mr. Wiesenthal and asked for his support. Mr. Wiesenthal promised that Pinkas will get 300 ATS and that his laundry will be taken care of, too. Ing. Wiesenthal, who brought Pinkas into misery, has thereby proved that he is ruthlessly willing to walk over corpses.

Now another case. The Mairovitsch couple lived as my neighbors in the Asten camp. Mr. Wiesenthal had a love affair with Mrs. Mairowitsch. When Mairowitsch got wind of this, he emigrated to Sweden with his wife. Herr Ing. Wiesenthal did not give up on his cause and sent love letters and parcels with chocolate and 100 dollar checks, american cigarettes etc. and asked the woman to break up with her husband and come to him. Mrs. Meirowitsch traveled to Austria. She had told her husband that she would be back in a few weeks. But after some time had passed and she had not returned to Sweden, Mr. Meirowitsch came to Asten to look for his wife. He visited me because he was once my neighbor and bemoaned his suffering. He had found his wife, but she had attempted suicide and was in Linz in the hospital of the barmherzige Brüder or barmh. Schwestern. Since Mr. Meirowitsch noticed that Wiesenthal was not willing to let Mairovitsch's wife go, he turned to the wife of Ing. Wiesenthal. Mr. Ing. Wiesenthal's answer was that he had Meirowitsch arrested by the security police and deported to Sweden via Bremen. Mairovitsch was tied up because Ing. Wiesenthal felt threatened by Meirovitsch. All this is known from a letter that Meirowitsch later wrote from Sweden and in which he reported everything.

One day in 1957, Mr. Wiesenthal came to my accommodation in the Asten camp and asked me for a "favour". For a long time he had been conducting a lawsuit against a former concentration camp kapo named Zimmermann, who lived in Linz and whom he wanted gone. Ing. Wiesenthal asked me to testify for him and state that I saw Zimmermann as a kapo in the concentration camp. When I said that I didn't know Zimmermann and that I hadn't been in Kraków but in a concentration camp near Kraków, Ing. Wiesenthal said that I should do him a favor and, against my better knowledge, make a statement in his favour. I was not inclined to do that and said to him that I would rather walk all the way to Linz than give false evidence in court, because, apart from the fact that I actually didn't know Zimmermann, I was reluctant to bring misfortune on him, since he was married and had children. I didn't want to burden my conscience with such an act. My refusal towards Ing. Wiesenthal seems to have spoiled the friendship.

After I was released, Mr. Wiesenthal put the tax office on me and they confiscated my books. I immediately suspected that Mr. Wiesenthal was behind this harassment. And this suspicion only became a certainty when the gentlemen from the tax office told me that I should go to the kultusgemeinde and compensate myself, otherwise I will no longer have peace in Asten. Another day, customs officials came to me, allegedly looking for smuggled American pants. These gentlemen also gave me the advice, unsolicited, that I should be reconciled with the kultusgemeinde. From this I can conclude that only Mr. Ing. Wiesenthal could be the man behind this harassment as well.

Everything I have described here is only the beginning. The main thing, however, is the affair of Mrs. Sabine Klapper and her son Moses. I have a letter from Mrs. Klapper that she sent to me from the US.

After my release, I was ill for about four weeks. I went to Vienna. There I met Mr. Fränkl. Mr. Fränkl said that he had heard about the misfortune that Ing. Wiesenthal had brought upon me. He suggested I go to the Israelite kultusgemeinde. Since the way there was too far for me, I thought it would be better to contact Dr. Blumenfeld, who is a member of the Kultusgemeinde. I asked Herr Fränkl to accompany me there. At Dr. Blumenfeld's office Mr. Fränkl stated Mr. Ing. W. was a heartless person. He described that Mrs. Zimmermann had been with Mr. Wiesenthal and had asked for the sake of her 2 children to be left alone. Mr Ing. Wiesenthal is said to have told her that if she wanted peace, she should jump from the highest floor in Linz with her two children, then she would have peace. This is what Mr. Fränkl said to Dr. Blumemfeld in my presence. At the same time he asked Dr. Blumenfeld not to tell Mr. Wiesenthal anything about this, since he, Fränkl, would otherwise have to fear for his reparation, since Mr. Wiesenthal could cause him great difficulties. A few days later I received a letter from Dr. Blumenfeld, in which he advised me to go to Mr. Wiesenthal and ask him to leave me alone. I still have that letter to this day. I was with Mr. Wiesenthal, who told me I should leave Asten, otherwise I will never have peace. Dr. Blumenfeld also wrote a letter to Mr. Wiesenthal.

Mrs. König, who lives in Asten, cried in front of Mr. Wiesenthal in his office in barrack 40, when her husband received an order from the Austrian government to leave the country within 14 days. She asked Mr. Wiesenthal for help until the emigration. Mr. Ing. Wiesenthal said cynically that the König family was none of his business and that one could do whatever one wanted with them.

The Bezirkshauptmann of Linz-Land, Kurt Hofinger, is an old illegal Nazi. His membership number is 6,371,884. He was a secretary during the Nazi era and a keen member of the so-called Säuberungs-Abteilung at Blum in Urfahr. Furthermore, Mr. Josef Hirzi from the Sicherheitsdirektion, also Mr. Anton Wimmer, the camp manager Mr. Karl Mayer and the head of the resettlement department, Mr. Reg. Rat Dr. Neweklowaki, all of these named persons supported Mr. Wiesenthal's position of power. He used them to exert his power.

Mr. Ing. Wiesenthal claims that I am not a concentration camp inmate. That's why he had me arrested. Now I have a letter from the public prosecutor of Walthut in Germany. According to this letter, I am to appear as a witness against war criminals. Mr. Wiesenthal provided my name. Oddly enough, in 1960 I am supposed to appear as a recognized concentration camp inmate, after Herr Ing. Wiesenthal had me arrested on November 18, 1959 because he stated that I was not a concentration camp inmate.

I learned Chimisch. In the Agdumois chapter it is written: even when the forests are made of feathers and the river is made of ink, one cannot describe what Mr Ing. Wiesenthal bears on his conscience.

The day before my release, Dr. Winter from Vienna called my wife and demanded bail of ATS 33,000.-, then I would be released from prison, otherwise I would remain in prison. My wife said that Herr Schreiber had already taken care of everything. Mr. Winter said that Mr. Schreiber couldn't help at all, if the S 33,000.- weren't deposited, I'd remain in custody. After my wife had told him that she had already given Mr. Markowski S 17,000.-, Mr. Winter confirmed this, but said that this was not enough, it must be S 50,000.-. When my wife said in tears that her husband's life was in great danger because of his illness, Dr. Winter stated that this was none of his concern. Then he added that I should not comment on this matter later and should not tell anyone.

Mr. Ing. Wiesenthal explained to me in his office that my arrest was not in his responsibility, he had previously spoken to his superior in Vienna, Mr. Krell, who he had agreed. I don't know a Mr. Krell at all and I don't believe a word that Mr. Ing. Wiesenthal, whose truthfulness I have every reason to doubt, spoke to Mr. Krell. Mr. Ing. Wiesenthal, as head of the Jewish Council, warned all refugees in the Asten camp not to associate with the Mandel family, otherwise he would stop the payments by the Joint as soon as possible. Where does Mr. Ing. Wiesenthal derive this arbitrary power from? Is the Joint money his personal property that he can freely dispose of? Is it his inheritance that he can distribute as he sees fit?
During my imprisonment, the Catholic pastor of Asten visited my wife.

He couldn't understand that Jews could act like that against their own brothers. When I suffered a nervous breakdown in prison in Steyr, the doctor was surprised that a sick person should be locked up. When I told him that I was an innocent victim of Mr. Wiesenthal from the Jewish community, he expressed his astonishment that the Brothers of Moses could act in this way. He had me transferred to the Inquisitenspital in Linz.

I earned my fortune honestly with blood and sweat from 1945 to 1959. Bezirksrat Hofinger had my goods confiscated at the request of Mr. Ing. Wiesenthal. These goods did not belong to me at all, but were given to me on commission by Viennese businessmen. To this day I am still burdened with it. My compensation, which I received in 1956 for the concentration camp imprisonment I suffered, was robbed from me, just as I was robbed in 1941 during the Nazi era. I don't have anything anymore, but the 10% I had to give as a commission are still there, but not with me. It is incomprehensible how Mr. Kurt Hofinger, who was in the Säuberungs-Abteilung during the Nazi era, can hold such a high post today. Why hasn't Herr Ing.Wiesenthal, who is known as an avid Nazi eater and Nazi persecutor, taken any action against Herr Hofinger yet? The solution to this question lies in the fact that Mr. Hofinger is a willing tool of Mr. Ing. Wiesenthal in pursuing his egoistic plans.

On the 4th day of my arrest, my wife and your mother was with you at Mr. Wiesenthal's. In tears she begged him for justice and asked why he had brought misery upon us. Mr. Ing. Wiesenthal said we were rich and should put a deposit of ATS 500,000.-, then I would be set free immediately; we had friends in Vienna who would help. [The] old Jewess Sabine Klapper from the US had brought the whole misfortune upon us. When your mother tearfully asked Mr. Ing. Wiesenthal to be fair, he opened the door and set the dog on you. This is exactly how the President of the Judenrat in the Jaworow Ghetto, Badjan, acted against his brothers in faith. If you ask me why the Judenrat could be like this, you can get an idea of how Mr. Ing. Wiesenthal acted in the good times and what a position of power he built up for himself. If he wants to take action against a Jew, he can also use an old Nazi. I was in a concentration camp and

I know what Säuberungsabteilung means. I would never have thought that after 14 years a Nazi would lock me up innocently again, and this time even on the orders of a Jew who, as chairman, was supposed to be our confidant and helper.

In order to provide me with clarification and truth, the Rabbi should mediate. I have the relevant letters. The Rabbi summoned Mr. Ing. Wiesenthal. He refused. I own the corresponding letter. I could put Mr. Ing. Wiesenthal in jail, just like he had me jailed. But my conscience won't allow me to bring misfortune on other people.

You ask me where my parents and siblings are. In your eyes I look like I was born from a stone. My parents and the youngest brother were gassed in Belz. Before the collapse, the two brothers were shot and burned. The whole family is on Lembergerstrasse under the Polish cemetery in the mass graves after the liquidation of the ghetto. The mass grave is in a field. When you have the opportunity, you will be able to convince yourself that all of this is true.

After the war, we concentration camp inmates fenced off the spot and erected a monument on which is written in Russian, Polish and Yiddish. Few victims survived. I myself had typhus fever in the ghetto in Jaworow, and I was hit on the head. Can you imagine that your father only weighed 36 kilos. I still have to bear the consequences of this suffering today. Because of this outrageous injustice, Mr. Ing. Wiesenthal arranged for me to get compensation. He said to me that if I give him 10% of it, then he can get me the quickest deal thanks to his good connections in Germany. The evidence of my concentration camp imprisonment, the papers that I handed Mr. Wiesenthal at that time (1953 or 1954) and which he considered as correct because he took the 10% commission, these same papers turned up in 1959 at the Sicherheitsdirektion again and this time Mr. Ing. Wiesenthal declared that they were fake.

Now you can see for yourself what kind of person Ing. Wiesenthal is. In front of the Joint, Mr. Ing. Wiesenthal explained that Moses Klapper, known as Sonny Boy, who lived in the Asten camp and was a sick person, received 1000.-, i.e. 650.- from the joint and 350.- from the Upper Austrian provincial government. In fact, the whole camp, Jews and Christians alike, knows that Moses Klapper ate in the camp kitchen. So where are the S 1000.- gone? Likewise, Mr. Ing. Wiesenthal stated at the Landesgendarmeriekommando in Linz that I received S 300.- from the Joint every month. That is a big lie. I didn't get a dime from the joint, on the contrary I paid cult tax and made donations to the State of Israel as well. I still have documents about it to this day. Mr. Ing. Wiesenthal wanted to put me down as a fraud with his report.

You ask me why in a neutral country you can throw an innocent person in prison despite being ill and can't give him medicine or linen. Now you can get an idea of how we lived back then under the Generalgouvernator Dr. Hans Frank (Krakow) in old Galicia, which once belonged to old Austria. Now you know what Judaism was like under such rule. I'm not filing an accusation, I just want to show that I was telling the truth. In Vienna there is still a company by the name Begovic, poultry and eggs, was stationed in Grodekjagellonski and Moszizka (Galicia), where it had two branches. My cousin Schaja Gerber and his wife Golda with 3 children were doused with petrol and burned with other Jews in the egg store of the company mentioned.

V e r m ä c h t n i s

An meine Söhne Abraham und Pimek, gegeben zu Wien im Jahre 1960.

Im Jahre 1953 oder 1954 wurde ich in die Baracke 40 des Lagers Asten
zu dem mir damals noch nicht bekannten Ing. Wiesenthal bestellt. Dieser
erklärte, daß er mir über die Uro eine Wiedergutmachung für erlittene
KZ-Haft beschaffen könne. Er verlangt Unterlagen für meine KZ-Haft, die
ich ihm übergab. Hierdurch wurde ich mit ihm näher bekannt. Im Jahre
1951 wohnte ich im Lager 1001 in Wels. In Wels wohnte damals ein mir
nicht näher bekannter Mann, von dem ich wußte, daß er im Besitze einer
japanischen Briefmarke war, die er gerne verkaufen wollte. Er frug mich,
ob ich ihm einen Interessenten hiefür nennen könne. Ich habe im Lager
Asten anderen Juden von dieser Marke erzählt. Diese haben an Herrn Ing.
Wiesenthal weiterberichtet und letzterer ließ mich eines Tages zu sich
in die Baracke 40 rufen. Dort hatte er eine Kanzlei als Direktor des
A.J.D.C. (Joint). Er bat mich, mit ihm in seinem Wagen zu dem Markenbe-
sitzer zu fahren und den Kauf zu vermitteln. Er wolle mich auch dafür
belohnen. Ich lehnte eine Belohnung ab, fuhr jedoch mit ihm mit und
kümmerte mich dann aber nicht mehr darum, ob der Kauf zu stande kam. So
kam die nähere Bekanntschaft zwischen Ing.Wiesenthal und mir zustande.
Im Jahre 1956 ließ mich Ing. Wiesenthal in seine Kanzlei nach Linz kommen. Dort teilte er mir mit, daß mein Ansuchen um Wiedergutmachung längere Zeit benötige, daß er aber gute Beziehungen habe und die Sache be-
schleunigen könne, wenn ich mich bereit erkläre, von der zu erwartenden
Summe 10 % an ihn abzutreten. Da ich damals dringend Geld benötigte, ging
ich auf seinen Vorschlag ein und das Geld wurde auch überwiesen. Damals
war er mein bester Freund. Ich bekam durch Einblicke in seine Gebahrung
und sein Verhalten gegenüber anderen Juden den Eindruck, daß er kein
guter Mensch sein kann, sondern ein Egoist, der nur auf seinen Vorteil
bedacht ist. Der Fall Pinkas Erdan zeigte mir dies: Pinkas Erdan war ein
Schwerkranker, der vom Joint monatlich S 600.- bekam. Eines Tages fiel
er bei Wiesenthal in Ungnade. Dieser ließ ihm, obgleich Pinkas ein schwerkranker Mensch war, die monatliche Unterstützung einstellen. Pinkas wandte
sich mit einem Schreiben an den Joint in Paris. Die Antwort des Ing.Wie-
senthal auf dieses Schreiben war eine Anzeige bei der Sicherheitsdirektion in Linz, nach welcher Pinkas ein Agent des Ostens sein soll, der
unter falschem Namen lebte. Pinkas wurde verhaftet und seien Papiere
wurden ihm angenommen. Als er nach wenigen Stunden wieder auf freien Fuß
gesetzt wurde, stand er ohne Dokumente da. Durch diesen Trick wollte Ing.
Wiesenthal verhindern, daß Pinkas, der ohne Papiere sich hilflos fühlte,

sich über ihn in Salzburg beschweren könne. Ich erfuhr dies alles durch Pinkas selber, der im Jahre 1958 im Krankenhaus Linz auf der Infektions- abteilung lag. Pinkas ließ mir damals durch einen ung. Flüchtling namens Hausner mitteilen, daß er koscher essen wolle. Ich habe ihm das von Haus- ner zubereitete Essen nach Linz ins Spital gebracht. Pinkas war sehr nie- dergeschlagen und weinte sehr und bat mich, ich solle zu Herrn Ing. Wiesen- thal gehen und ihn bitten, daß er ihm wieder eine Unterstützung zukommen lassen solle. Ich bin zu Herrn Ing. Wiesenthal gegangen und habe für Pin- kas gebeten. Herr Ing. Wiesenthal hat zugesagt, daß Pinkas 300.- S bekommt und außerdem für seigne Wäsche gesorgt würde. Ing. Wiesenthal, der Pinkas ins Elend gebracht hat, hat dadurch bewiesen, daß er rücksichtslos auch über Leichen zu gehen bereit ist.

Nun ein anderer Fall. Im Lager Asten lebte als mein Nachbar das Ehepaar Mairowitsch. Herr Ing. Wiesenthal unterhielt mit der Frau Mairowitsch ein Liebesverhältnis. Als Mairowitsch hiervon Wind bekam, wanderte er mit seiner Frau nach Schweden aus. Herr Ing. Wiesenthal gab seine Sache nicht verloren und schickte Liebesbriefe und Päckchen mit Schokolade und 100- Dollar-Schecks, Ami-Zigaretten usw. und bat die Frau, sich von ihrem Mann zu trennen und zu ihm zu kommen. Frau Mairowitsch reiste nach Österreich. Ihrem Mann hatte sie gesagt, daß sie in wenigen Wochen zurückkehren werde. Nachdem aber längere Zeit verstrichen war und sie nicht nach Schweden zu- rückgekehrt war, kam Herr Mairowitsch nach Asten, um seine Frau zu suchen. Er besuchte mich, weil er einmal mein Nachbar war und klagte mir sein Leid. Er hatte seine Frau gefunden, doch diese hatte einen Selbstmordversuch gemacht und lag in Linz im Spital der Barmherzigen Brüder /oder Barmh. Schwestern. Da Herr Mairowitsch merkte, daß Herr Ing. Wiesenthal nicht gewillt war, Mairowitsch's Frau zu lassen, wandte sich dieser an die Ehe- frau des Ing. Wiesenthal. Die Antwort des Herrn Ing. Wiesenthal war, daß er Mairowitsch durch die Sicherheitspolizei verhaften ließ und über Bremen nach Schweden abschieben ließ. Mairowitsch war gefesselt, da Ing. Wiesen- thal sich durch Mairowitsch bedroht fühlte. Dies weiß man durch einen Brief den Mairowitsch später aus Schweden geschrieben hatte und in dem er alles berichtet hatte.

Im Jahre 1957 kam eines Tages Herr Ing. Wiesenthal zu mir in meine Woh- nung im Lager Asten und ersuchte mich um eine "Gefälligkeit". Er führte schon seit längerem einen Prozess gegen einen ehemaligen KZ-Kapo namens Zimmermann, der in Linz wohnte und den er weg haben wollte. Ing. Wiesenthal ersuchte mich, ich solle für ihn einen Zeugen machen und angeben, daß ich Zimmermann als Kapo im KZ gesehen habe. Als ich sagte, daß ich Zimmermann nicht kenne und daß ich nicht in Krakau, sondern in einem KZ bei Krakau gewesen war, meinte Ing. Wiesenthal, daß ich doch ihm den Gefallen tun sol- le und wider besseres Wissen eine Aussage zu seinen Gunsten machen. Ich war dazu nicht geneigt und sagte zu ihm, lieber wolle ich zu Fuß nach Linz gehen als eine unrichtige Aussage vor Gericht machen, denn, abgesehen da- von, daß ich Zimmermann wirklich nicht kannte, widerstrebte es mir, ihm

ins Unglück zu bringen, da er verheiratet war und Kinder hatte. Ich wollte
mein Gewissen nicht mit solcher Tat belasten. Meine Weigerung gegenüber
Ing. Wiesenthal hat anscheinend die Freundschaft verdorben.

Nach meiner Enthaftung schickte mir Herr Ing. Wiesenthal das Finanzamt
auf den Hals, das meine Bücher beschlagnahmte. Ich vermutete gleich, daß
hinter dieser Schikane Herr Ing. Wiesenthal steckte. Und diese Vermutung
wurde zur Gewißheit, als die Herren vom Finanzamt zu mir sagten, ich solle
zur Kultusgemeinde gehen und mich ausgleichen, sonst würde ich keine Ruhe
mehr in Asten haben. Eines anderen Tages kamen Beamte des Zolls zu mir
und suchten angeblich geschmuggelte amerikanische Hosen. Auch diese Herrn
gaben mir unaufgefordert den Rat, ich solle mich mit der Kultusgemeinde
aussöhnen. Daraus kann ich schließen, daß auch hinter dieser Schikane nur
Herr Ing. Wiesenthal steht.

Alles, was ich hier geschildert habe, ist nur der Auftakt. Die Hauptsache
ist jedoch die Angelegenheit der Frau Sabine Klapper und ihres Sohnes Moses.
Ich besitze ein Schreiben der Frau Klapper, das sie mir aus USA geschickt
hat.

Nach meiner Enthaftung war ich ca. 4 Wochen krank. Ich fuhr nach Wien. Dort
traf ich Herrn Fränkl. Herr Fränkl erzählte mir, daß er von dem Unglück, wel
ches Herr Ing. Wiesenthal über mich gebracht hat, gehört habe. Er schlug mir
vor, zur Israelitischen Kultusgemeinde zu gehen. Da mir der Weg dorthin zu
weit war, hielt ich es für besser, Herrn Dr. Blumenfeld, der ja Mitglied
der Kultusgemeinde ist, aufzusuchen. Ich bat Herrn Fränkl, mich dorthin zu
begleiten. Bei Herrn Dr. Blumenfeld erzählte Herr Fränkl, daß Herr Ing. W.
ein herzloser Mensch sei. Er schilderte, daß die Frau Zimmermann bei Herrn
Ing. Wiesenthal gewesen sei und um ihrer 2 Kinder willen gebeten habe, in
Ruhe gelassen zu werden. Herr Ing. Wiesenthal soll zu ihr gesagt haben,
wenn sie Ruhe wolle, so solle sie mit ihren 2 Kindern vom höchsten Stock-
werk in Linz hinunterstürzen, dann werde sie Ruhe haben. Dies sagte Herr
Fränkl in meiner Gegenwart zu Herrn Dr. Blumenfeld. Gleichzeitig bat er
Herrn Dr. Blumenfeld, hierüber gegenüber Herrn Ing. Wiesenthal nichts zu
verlauten, da er, Fränkl ansonsten um seine Wiedergutmachung fürchten müsse,
da ihm Herr Ing. Wiesenthal größte Schwierigkeiten machen könne. Einige Tage
später bekam ich einen Brief von Herrn Dr. Blumenfeld, in dem er mir riet
zu Herrn Ing. Wiesenthal zu gehen und ihn zu bitten, daß er mich in Ruhe
lasse. Diesen Brief habe ich heute noch. Ich war bei Herrn Ing Wiesenthal,
dieser sagte zu mir, ich solle Asten verlassen, sonst werde ich nie Ruhe
haben. Herr Dr. Blumenfeld hat auch an Herrn Ing. Wiesenthal geschrieben.
Die Frau König, wohnhaft Asten, ~~kurzkurzkurz~~ weinte vor Herrn Ing. Wiesenth
in dessen Büro in der Baracke 40, als deren Mann durch die österr. Regierun
die Aufforderung erhielt, binnen 14 Tagen das Land zu verlassen. Sie bat
Herrn Ing. Wiesenthal um Hilfe bis zur Auswanderung. Herr Ing. Wiesenthal
sagte zynisch, daß ihn die Familie König nichts angehe, man könne mit ihr
machen, was man wolle.

Der Bezirkshauptmann von Linz-Land, ~~Hofinger~~ Kurt Hofinger ist ein alter illegaler Nazi. Seine Mitgliedsnummer ist 6,371,884. Er war ein Sekretär in der Nazizeit und ein eifiges Mitglied der sog. Säuberungs-Abteilung, beim Blum in Urfahr. Weiteres der Herr Josef ~~Hirzi~~ Hirzi von der Sicherheitsdirektion, ferner Herr Anton Wimmer, der Lagerleiter Herr Karl Mayer und der Leiter der Abteilung Umsiedlung, Herr Reg.Rat Dr. Neweklowski, alle diese genannten Personen stützen die Machtposition des Herrn Ing.Wiesenthal. Er bedient sich ihrer, um seine Macht auszuüben.

Herr Ing.Wiesenthal behauptet, daß ich kein KZler sei. Deshalb hat er mich verhaften lassen. Nunbesitze ich ein Schreiben des Staatsanwaltes von Waldhut in Deutschland. Nach diesem Schreiben soll ich als Zeuge gegen Kriegsverbrecher auftreten. Namhaft gemacht hat mich Herr Ing.Wiesenthal. Merkwürdigerweise soll ich nun, im Jahre 1960 als anerkannter KZ-Ler auftreten, nachdem Herr Ing.Wiesenthal am 18.11.59 mich noch verhaften ließ, da er angab, ich sei kein KZ-ler gewesen.

Ich habe ~~einmal~~ Chimisch gelernt. Im Kapitel Agdumois steht geschrieben: wenn die Wälder sind aus Pennen und der Fluß ist aus Tinte, kann man nicht beschreiben, was Herr Ing.Wiesenthal auf seinem Gewissen hat.

Einen Tag vor meiner Enthaftung rief Herr Dr. Winter aus Wien meine Frau an und verlangte eine Kaution von S 33,000.-, dann würde ich aus der Haft entlassen, widrigenfalls bleibe ich verhaftet. Meine Frau sagte, daß Herr Schreiber doch schon alles erledigt habe. Herr Winter sagte, daß Herr Schreiber garnicht helfen könne, wenn die 33,000.- S nicht erlegt werden, bleibe ich weiter in Haft. Nachdem meine Frau ihm gesagt hatte, daß sie Herrn Markowski bereits S 17,000.- gegeben habe, bestätigte dies Herr Winter, meinte aber, daß das nicht genug sei, es müssen 50,000.- S sein. Als meine Frau unter Tränen sagte, daß ihr Mann wegen seiner Krankheit in höchster Lebensgefahr schwebe, meinte Herr Dr.Winter, daß ihn das nicht interessiere Dann fügte er hinzu, ich solle mich über diese Sache später nicht weiter äußern und niemanden etwas erzählen.

Herr Ing.Wiesenthal erklärte mir in seiner Kanzlei, daß meine Verhaftung nicht auf seine Verantwortung erfolgt sei, er habe vorher mit seinem Chef in Wien, Herrn Kroll gesprochen und dieser habe zugestimmt. Mir ist ein Herr Kroll gänzlich unbekannt und glaube ich kein Wort, daß Herr Ing.Wiesenthal, an dessen Wahrhaftigkeit zu zweifeln ich allen Grund habe, mit Herrn Kroll gesprochen habe. Herr Ing.Wiesenthal hat als Oberster des Judenrates alle Flüchtlinge im Lager Asten gewarnt, mit der Familie Mandl zu verkehren widrigenfalls er ihnen die Joint-Unterstützung auf schnellstem Wege einstellen werde. Woraus leitet Herr Ing.Wiesenthal diese Eigenmächtigkeit ab. Ist das Joint-Geld sein persönliches Eigentum, über das er frei verfügen kann? Ist es sein Erbe, das er nach eigenem Gutdünken verteilen kann? Während meiner Haft hatte der katholische Pfarrer von Asten meine Frau besucht. Er konnte es nicht begreifen, daß Juden so gegen ihre Mitbrüder handeln können. Als ich im Gefängnis in Steyr einen Nervenzusammenbruch

erlitt, wunderte sich der Arzt, daß man einen kranken Menschen einsperren läßt. Als ich ihm sagte, daß ich ein unschuldiges Opfer des Herrn
Ing.Wiesenthal von der Israelitischen Kultusgemeinde sei, äußerte er
seine Verwunderung darüber, daß die Brüder Moses so handeln können.
Er ließ mich in das Linzer inquisitenspital überstellen.
Mein Vermögen habe ich mir von 1945 bis 1959 ehrlich mit Blut und
Schweiß erarbeitet. Herr Bezirkshauptmann Hofinger hat mx über Auftrag
von Herrn Ing.Wiesenthal meine Ware beschlagnehemn lassen. Dabei gehörte
diese Ware garnicht mir, sondern war mir von Wiener Geschäftsleuten in
Kommission gegeben. Nun bin ich bis zum heutigen Tage noch damit belaste
Meine Wiedergutmachung, die ich 1956 für erlittene KZ-Haft erhielt, hat
man mir ausgeplündert, genau wie man mich ausgeraubt hat 1941 in der inx
Nazizeit. Ich habe nichts mehr, aber die 10 %, die ich habe als Provisio
geben müssen, die sind noch da, aber nicht bei mir. Unbegreiflich ist
wieso der Herr Kurt Hofinger, der doch in der Nazizeit bei der Säuberun
Abteilung war, heute einen so hohen Posten bekleiden kann. Weshalb hat
Herr Ing.Wiesenthal, der doch ein eifriger Nazifresser und Naziver-
folger ist, noch nichts gegen Herrn Hofinger unternommen. Die Lösung
dieser Frage liegt darin, , daß Herr Hofinger ein williges Werkzeug
des Herrn Ing.Wiese thal ist bei der Verfolgung von dessen egoistischen
Plänen. Am 4.Tag nach meiner Verhaftung war meine Frau, Eure Mutter mit
Euch bei Herrn Ing.Wiesenthal. Unter Tränen bat sie ihn um Gerechtig-
keit und fragte, weshalb er uns ins Unglück gestürzt habe,. Herr Ing.
Wiesenthal meinte, wir seien reich und sollten S 500,000.- Kaution
stellen, dann würde ich sofort entlassen; wir hätten Freunde in Wien,
die würden helfen. Das ganze Unglück habe alte Jüdin Sabine Klapper aus
USA über uns gebracht. . Als Eure Mutter unter Tränen Herrn Ing.Wiesen-
thal bat, gerecht zu sein, öffnete er die Tür und hetzte den Hund auf
Euch. Genau so hat der Präsident des Judenrates im Ghetto Jaworow,
Radjan, gegen seine Glaubensbrüder gehandelt, enn Ihr mich fragt, wieso der Judenrat so sein konte, so könnt Ihr Euch ein Bild machen, wie
Herr Ing.Wiesenthal in der guten zeit handelt und was für eine Machtposition er sich aufbaut. Wenn er gegen einen Juden vorgehen will,
dann kann er sich auch eines alten Nazis bedienen. Ich war im KZ uns weiß
weiß was Säuberungsabteilung bedeutet. Ich hätte nie gedacht, daß nach
14 Jahren wieder ein Nazi mich unschuldigerweise einsperren wird, und
diesmal noch sogar auf Befehl eines Juden, der doch als Obmann unser
Vertrauensmann und Helfer sein sollte.
Um mir Klärung und Wahrheit zu verschaffen, sollte der Herr Rabbiner
vermitteln. Ich besitze die diesbezüglichen Schreiben. Der Herr Rabbiner
hat Herrn Ing.Wiesenthal vorgeladen. Dieser hat es abgelehnt. Das Schreiben besitze ich. Ich könnte Herrn Ing.Wiesenthal ins Gefängnis bringen,
genau so, wie er mich hat einsperren lassen. Aber mein Gewissen erlaubt

es mir nicht, daß ich andere Leute ins Unglück bringe.

Ihr fragt mich, wo meine Eltern und Geschwister sind. In Euren Augen schaue ich aus, wie aus einem Stein geboren. Meine Eltern und den jüngsten Bruder hat man in XX Belz vergast. Vor dem Zusammenbruch hat man die beiden Brüder erschossen und verbrannt. Die ganze Familie befindet sich auf der Lembergerstraße unter dem polnischen Friedhof in den Massengräbern nach der Liquidation des Ghettos. Das Massengrab befindet sich auf einem Feld. Wenn Ihr die Möglichkeit haben werdet, so werdet Ihr Euch überzeugen können, daß dies alles Wahrheit ist. Wir KZ-ler haben nach dem Krieg den Platz umzäunt und ein Denkmal gesetzt, auf dem in russischer, polnischer und jiddischer Sprache geschrieben steht. Nur wenige Opfer haben überlebt. Ich selber hatt Flecktyphus durchgemacht im Ghetto in Jaworow, auf den Kopf bekam ich einen Schlag. Könnt Ihr Euch vorstellen, daß Euer Vater nur 36 kg gewogen hat. Unter den Folgen dieser Leiden habe ich heute noch zu tragen. Auf Grund dieses himmelschreienden Unrechtes hat mir Herr Ing.Wiesenthal die Wiedergutmachung besorgt. Er hat zu mir gesagt, wenn ich ihm 10 % davon ablasse, dann verschafft er mir durch seine guten Beziehungen in Deutschland die zucke schnellste Erledigung. Die Beweise für meine KZ-Haft, die Papiere, die ich Herrn Ing.Wiesenthal damals gegeben habe (1953) oder 1954) und die er richtig ansah, weil er doch die 10% Provision nahm, diese gleichen Papiere tauchten im Jahre 1959 bei der Sicherheitsdirektion wieder auf und diesmal erklärte Herr Ing.Wiesenthal, sie seien gefälscht.

Nun macht Euch selbst ein Bild, was für ein Mensch der Ing.Wiesenthal ist. Vor dem Joint hat Herr Ing.Wiesenthal erklärt, daß der im Lager Asten wohnhafte Moses Klapper, genannt Sonny Boy, ein kranker Mensch, 1000.—, dh. vom Joint 650,— und von der oberösterreichischen Landesregierung S 350.— erhalten hat. In Wirklichkeit weiß das ganze Lager, Juden wie Christen, daß Moses Klapper in der Lagerküche gegessen hat. Wo sind also die S 1000.— geblieben? Ebenso gab Herr Ing.Wiesenthal beim Landesgendarmeriekommando in Linz an, ich habe vom Joint jeden Monat S 300.— erhalten. Das ist eine große Lüge. Ich habe vom Joint nicht einen Groschen bekommen, im Gegenteil habe ich Kultussteuer gezahlt und außerdem Spenden für den Staat Israel getätigt. Unterlagen hierüber besitze ich noch heute. Ing.Wiesenthal wollte mich durch seine Anzeige als Betrüger hinstellen.

Ihr fragt mich, wieso man in einem neutralen Land einen unschuldigen Menschen trotz Krankheit ins Gefängnis werfen kann und ihm weder Medikamente noch Wäsche geben kann. Nun könnt Ihr Euch ein Bild machen wie wir gelebt haben damals unter dem Generalgouvernator Dr. Hans Frank (Krakau) im alten Galizien, das früher einmal zum alten Österreich gehört hat. Jetzt wißt Ihr, wie das Judentum unter solcher Herrschaft ausgesehen hat. Ich mache keine Anzeige, sondern will nur aufweisen, daß ich die Wahrheit gesagt habe. In Wien lebt noch eine Firma Begovic, Geflügel und Eier, war stationiert in Grodekjagellonski und Moszizka (Galizien), wo er zwei Niederlassungen hatte. Mein Cousin Schaja Gerber und seine Frau Golda mit 3 Kindern wurden (im Eiermagazin) mit anderen Juden der genannten Firma mit Benzin übergossen und verbrannt worden.

Further documents:

Instigation Hofrat Dr. Hoffinger

commissioned by Simon Wiesenthal.

Echo-Chefreporter Peter Gottfried Eder deckt auf:

HOFRAT KNACK

Echo beweist: Hofrat Hofinger im „Illegalenblock" — „Registrierwunder" um Dr. Kurt brachte zweite Klage ein — Landeskreise sagen: „Diese Verfahren werd

Hofrat Dr. Kurt Hofinger, Bezirkshauptmann von Linz-Land und Staatskommissär der Ennser Sparkasse, zeigte sich vor kurzem überrascht, als ihm vom Bezirksgericht in Enns mitgeteilt wurde, daß Sparkassendirektor Max Neundlinger nunmehr aus „allen „Rohren" zu schießen beginnt. Neundlinger hat gegen den Staatskommissär bekanntlich beim Bezirksgericht in Linz die Klage wegen Ehrenbeleidigung eingebracht. Der Herr Hofrat hat dem Sparkassendirektor vorgehalten, daß er eine bestimmte Kredittransaktion entweder nur machte, weil er möglicherweise korrupt oder zu dumm war, um die Folgen zu überblicken. Vorwürfe, die natürlich schwer wiegen, weil diese Anschuldigungen seitens des Herrn Hofrates auch dem gesamten Vorstand gegenüber gemacht und somit auf ein anderes Forum ausgedehnt wurden, klagte Neundlinger neuerlich, diesmal in Enns.

Die Auflehnung des jungen und ambitionierten Sparkassendirektors gegen Hofinger hat vielbeachtete Anerkennung sogar in Kreisen gefunden, die mit dieser Angelegenheit auch nicht entfernt etwas zu tun haben. Auch uns gingen zahlreiche Zuschriften zu, in denen man Echo gratulierte. All diese Briefe spiegeln merkwürdigerweise e i n Symptom wider: Man wirft Hofinger eine Wandelbarkeit im Zeitlauf zweier Jahrzehnte vor.

Der Autor dieser Berichte hatte wiederholt die Möglichkeit, mit Hofinger zu sprechen. Man ist geneigt, sich beeindruckt zu zeigen von seiner (sagen wir) Wendigkeit der Ausdrucksweise und der Betrachtung verschiedener für ihn persönlich heikler Probleme. Sein Verhalten während jener denkwürdigen Besprechung im Direktionszimmer der Ennser Sparkasse offenbarte, daß Hofinger auch vor einem größeren Forum bereit ist, „einzustecken", wenn er glaubt, daß diese Defensivtaktik im Augenblick besser für ihn und seinen Stand ist.

Hofinger und die Registrierungspflicht

Wir erinnern uns alle, wie es 1945 war: Jeder auch nur ganz am Rande mit der NSDAP zu tun hatte, wurde durch die Registrierungs- und Entnazifizierungsmaschine gedreht. Tausende Existenzen kleiner, unbedeutender NS-Parteimitglieder wurden zermahlen. Familien standen vor dem Nichts, weil der Ernährer in näherem oder fernerem Zusammenhang mit der NSDAP stand. Aber es gab auch einige wenige, die es verstanden, sich aus dieser harten Mühle herauszuhalten ...

Echo hätte dieses Problem nicht aufgezeigt, wenn nicht der Herr Hofrat von sich aus dazu förmlich aufgefordert hätte. Hofinger ließ uns wissen, daß er nicht illegales Mitglied der NSDAP war. Das haben wir auch niemals aus einem Satz seines Zusammenhanges des Gesamtgefüges.

Aber etwas ließ Hofinger uns auch wissen, und das überrascht uns. „Ich war weder illegales Mitglied der NSDAP, noch war ich registrierungspflichtig." Das hieß: Hofinger war auch nicht ordentliches Mitglied der NSDAP. Nun, hier wollen wir dem Gedächtnis des derzeitigen Bezirkshauptmannes von Linz-Land etwas nachhelfen.

Am 2. Mai 1938 veröffentlichte die „Tages-Post" in ihrem Mittagsblatt auf Seite 4 folgende Bekanntmachung, die wir vollinhaltlich veröffentlichen wollen:

Mitgliedaufnahme zur NSDAP
Bisherige Mitglieder und Nationalsozialisten der Tat

Der Beauftragte des Führers, Gauleiter Bürckel, hat mit der Erfassung und Aufnahme der Mitglieder zur NSDAP die Gauwahlleiter beauftragt. Auf Grund der ergangenen Anordnung werden als Mitglieder der NSDAP erfaßt und aufgenommen:

1. Diejenigen, die b i s h e r Mitglieder der NSDAP waren.

2. Jene, die bis zum 11. März 1938 sich als Nationalsozialisten betätigt haben und durch ihre nationalsozialistische Betätigung mit die Voraussetzung zu der Entwicklung des 11. März geschaffen haben.

Dies geschieht in der Weise, daß den Ortsgruppenleitern der Auftrag erteilt wird, diese beiden Gruppen zu erfassen. Es hat jeder einen Antrag auf Ausstellung einer vorläufigem Mitgliedskarte auszufüllen. Diesem Antrag ist ein vorgeschriebener Fragebogen ausgefüllt beizugeben."

Das war, wie jederzeit nachgelesen werden kann, am 2. Mai 1938.

Für Hofrat Dr. Hofinger hatte das keine Gültigkeit mehr. Er rückte, seinen eigenen Angaben folgend, am 27. August 1939 ein. Am 12. Oktober 1940 war seine Soldatenzeit beendet. Er erkrankte in Frankreich an einer Ruhr. In der weiteren Folge war er dem Landrat zugeteilt. Monate hindurch war er jedoch, weil der Landrat selbst verreist war, mit den Agenden dieser Funktion geschäftsführend betraut. Es war schon immer verwunderlich, wenn Hofinger zu verstehen gab, mit der NSDAP recht wenig gemeinsam gehabt zu haben.

Nun, im Jahre 1938 scheint das noch nicht ganz der Fall gewesen zu sein. In Linz gibt es nämlich noch etliche Bürger, die sich erinnern, wie Hofinger zur NSDAP stieß. Echo will heute auch Hofingers NSDAP-Mitgliedsnummer veröffentlichen.

Sie lautet: 6.371.884, Mitglied seit 1. Mai 1938

Bekanntlich würden von den Volksgerichten alle Mitgliedsnummern, die unter der Grenze 6,400.000 lagen, als Illegalenblock bezeichnet. Das heißt: Man nahm an, daß die Träger jener Mitgliedsnummern unter 6,4 Millionen illegal waren. Es soll ja damals im Jahre 1938 auch zahlreiche Bewerber gegeben haben, die

Echo **die österreichische Nachrichtenillustrierte**

Herausgeber: Gustaf Adolf Neumann, Eigentümer und Verleger: Verlag Gustaf Ad Telegrammadresse (Telex): Echo-Wien. Postscheckkonto Wien 187.086. Chefredakteur Seidengasse 11, Telephon 93 36 45, Fernschreiber 01 1935. Zentralvertrieb und Zentral gasse 12, Telephon 35 43 71 (für Wien und Niederösterreich); L i n z, Stockbauernstraße b u r g, Mayburger Kai 28, Telephon 75 6 66, 75 6 67, Fernschreiber 06 414; E i s e r Burgenland; I n n s b r u c k, Andreas-Hofer-Straße 40, Telephon 70 5 46, Fernschreiber 05 390; B r e g e n z, Lindauerstraße 16, F K l a g e n f u r t, Völkermarktstraße 53/l, Telephon 35 92, Fernschreiber 04 217. Verantwortlich für den Textteil: Jaro Hochmann; Gesellschaft m.b.H., Wien VII, Neubaugasse 40, Telephon 93 23 25. Technische Herstellung im Lohndruck bei Waldheim-Eberle, Manuskripteinsendungen und Unterlagen übernimmt der Verlag keine Haftung. Rücksendung nur, wenn Rückporto beiliegt. Nac postamt Wien 62. P. b.

(VII)

...urt Hofinger — Direktor Neundlinger
...erden wichtig sein"

...en, man möge ihnen „eine gute Nummer"
...en (heute gibt es so etwas auch bei Auto-
...nzeichen). Hofinger jedenfalls war Träger
...er „guten Nummer".

...Man würde sich täuschen, wenn man an-
...me, daß Hofinger nach dem Zusammen-
...ch der NSDAP unter den Gemaßregelten

Hofrat Dr. Kurt Hofinger

...finden war. Ganz im Gegenteil. Er selbst
...stieg dem Chaos wirklich wie Phönix aus
...Asche und war wieder zu bewundern:
...n Staatsbeauftragtenstellvertreter Doktor
...m in Urfahr. Hier fungierte er als dessen
...retär. Man weiß, daß Dr. Blum auch mit
...Agenden der politischen Säuberung be-
...t war und sein Amt recht genau ausübte.
...nger wird ihm dabei als Sekretär gewiß
... dienlich gewesen sein.

...och haben wir das uns angebotene Ma-
...al nicht ganz auf die Richtigkeit unter-
...t. Heute nur soviel: Der von Hofinger an-
...gte Entregistrierungsakt, der trotz gegen-
...ger Behauptungen von ihm vorhanden ist,
...t eine Flut von Bescheinigungen auf, daß
...Herr Hofrat sich wiederholt als Gegner
...NS-Regimes bewährt und zu erkennen
...ben habe.

...af Adolf Neumann, Wien VII, Seidengasse 11, Telephon 93 36 45.
...dakteur: Gustaf Adolf Neumann. Zentralredaktion: Wien VII,
...entralverwaltung: L i n z, Stockbauerstraße 11, Telephon 22 3 77,
...straße 11, Telephon 27 5 64. Redaktionsbüros: W i e n II, Floß-
...auernstraße 11, Telephon 22 7 16, Fernschreiber 02 153; S a l z-
...i s e n s t a d t, St. Georgnerstraße 2. Telephon 27 82 (für das
... 16, Postfach 244. Telephon 40 5 22; G r a z : Plüddemannstraße 19. Telephon 33 1 91. Fernschreiber 04 377;
...anny für den Inseratenteil: Erna Riehs, beide Wien VII, Seidengasse 11. Klischees: Klischeeanstalt Neumann,
...berle, Großdruckerei und Verlagshaus Dr. Ludwig Polsterer, Wien VII, Seidengasse 3—11. Bedingungen: Für
... Nachdruck nur mit Genehmigung des Chefredakteurs und mit Quellenangabe. Erscheinungsort Wien, Verlags-
...P. b. b.

Echo **ist frei von jeder Parteipolitik**

A b s c h r i f t

Z 163/59

H a f t b e f e h l

Herrn

Szulim M a n d l, geb. 2o.3.19o7, Kaufmann in Asten
Wohnsiedlung Nr. 117, Bar. 25/27

Es ergeht hiemit der Auftrag, Sie in Haft zu nehmen, weil Sie
verdächtig sind, das Verbrechen des Betruges, der Verleitung zum
Missbrauche der Amtsgewalt und der Übertretung der Irreführung der
öffentlichen Aufsicht na §§ 197 ff,1o5,32o a StG., dadurch begangen z
zu haben, weil Sie durch falsche Angaben über Ihre ehemalige Staatsbürgerschaft, Ihre Herkunft, Ihren Beruf und Ihren Taufnamen die
öffentliche Aufsicht in Irrtum geführt und auf Grund Ihrer falschen
Angabe polnischer Flüchtling zu sein, in der Zeit vom März 1952 bis
3o.6.1955 zu Unrecht von der Bundesrepublik Österreich Fürsorgeunterstützung bezogen und dadurch die Bundesrepublik Österreich um
ca. S 24.ooo.- geschädigt haben. Weiters besteht der Verdacht, dass
Sie durch Zahlung von Bestechungsgeldern an Beamt der Bezirkshauptmannschaft Linz-Land das Verbrechen der Verleitung zum Missbrauche
der Amtsgewalt begangen haben.

Der im § 175 Zl. 2, 3 StPO. bezeichnete Haftgrund liegt vor,
weil Sie wegen der Grösse der Ihnen mutmasslich bevorstehenden Strafe
der Flucht verdächtig sind und weil Sie eine die Ermittlung der
Wahrheit hindernde Art auf Zeugen oder Mitbeschuldigte einwirken
könnten.

Bezirksgericht Enns
am 18.Nov.1959

Dr. Krein eh.

ZV

1) 2fach an
Sicherheitsdion Linz

Abgef. 1o.Nov. 1959.

A b s c h r i f t   Z 163/59
                                    5

Hausdurchsuchungsbefehl

In der Strafsache gegen Szulim Mandl wegen §§ 1o5.197 ff,
32o a StG. wird die Erhebungsexpositur bei der Sicherheitsdirektion
für das Bundesland Österreich in Linz ermächtigt, in der Wohnung
des Beschuldigten Szulim Mandl, Kaufmann in Asten b. Enns, WS 117,
Bar. 25/27 eine Hausdurchsuchung vorzunehmen.

       G r ü n d e :

Der Beschuldigte Szulim Mandl ist dringend verdächtig, das
Verbrechen der Verleitung zum Missbrauche der Amtsgewalt nach
§ 1o5 StG., das Verbrechen des Betruges nach §§ 197 ff StG. und die
Übertretung der Irreführung der öffentlichen Aufsicht nach : 32o a
StG. dadurch begangen zu haben, weil er Bestechungsgelder an Beamte
der Bezirkshauptmannschaft Linz-Land gezahlt haben soll, weiters
weil er auf Grund seiner falschen Angabe polnischer Flüchtling zu
sein, in der Zeit vom März 1952 bis 3o.6.1955 zu Unrecht von der
Bundesrepublik Österreich Fürsorgeunterstützung im Betrage von
ca. S 24.ooo.- bezogen hat und ferner durch falsche Angaben über
seine ehemalige Staatsbürgerschaft etc. die öffentliche Aufsicht
im Irrtum geführt hat.

Da der Verdacht besteht, dass der Beschuldigte Dokumente und
Aufzeichnungen, die sich in seiner Wohnung befinden und die zur
Klärung der dem Beschuldigten zur Last gelegten strafbaren Handlungen von grosser Wichtigkeit sind, beiseite schaffen könnte, war
die Hausdurchsuchung ohne vorherige Einvernahme anzuordnen.

                    Bezirksgericht Enns
                    am 18.Nov. 1959
ZV: Dr. Krein eh.
1.) 2fach an
    Sicherheitsdion Linz

          V.
    Pflichtanzeige an St. A. Steyr abfertigen.
                              Enns 18.11.1959
Abgef. 18.11.1959

103

AMBASSADE D' ISRAEL
44/937

Wien, 23.11.1959

An die
Sicherheitsdirektion f.d.Bdl. O.Oe.
in Linz

Betr.: M a n d e l Szulim, geb. 2o.3.19o7 - Staatsbürgerschaft

Die Konsularabteilung der Botschaft des Staates Israel bestätigt den
Empfang des werten Schreibens vom 2o.ds.M.,Zl. 14.168/59 und beehrt sich
mitzuteilen, dass zur authentischen Feststellung der Staatsbürgerschaft
eine Rückfrage in Jerusalem nötig erscheint.
Herr Szulim Mandel könnte theoretisch die israelische Staatsbürgerschaft
besitzen, trotzdem er nur mit einem Reiseausweis (Passersatz) aus Israel
ausreiste.
Die Konsularabteilung wird es nicht versäumen, sofort über die eingelaufene
Antwort die Sicherheitsdirektion zu verständigen und benützt den Anlass,
ihre vorzügliche Hochachtung zu erneuern.

F.d.R.d.A.
    Wagner eh.

M. Dak
Erster Sekretär eh.

Abschrift.

Ambassade D'ISRAEL

416o

Die Konsularabteilung der Botschaft des Staates Israel beehrt sich
im Nachtrage zu ihrem Schreiben vom 23.11.1959 mitzuteilen, dass Herr
Mandel Szulim, geb.am 2o.3.19o7, die israelische Staatsbürgerschaft
nicht erworben hat.
Die Konsularabteilung der Botschaft des Staates Israel erneuert bei
diesem Anlass den Ausdruck ihrer vorzüglichen Hochachtung.

Wien,1.März 196o

M. Dak Botschaftssekretär eh.

An die
Sicherheitsdirektion f.d.Bdl. O.Oe.
Linz

F.d.R.d.A.

    Wagner eh.

Letter to the

Joint Distribution Committee

(1961).

Schulim M a n d e l
Wien,2.,Josefinengasse 6/11

Wien, 28. Oktober 1961

An das
American JOINT Distribution Committee

W i e n , 9 . ,
Währingerstr. 2 - 4

In meiner verzweifelten Lage, in die mich, zusammen mit meiner
Familie, Ihr Vertreter in Linz, Herr Ing. Wiesenthal, gestürzt hat,
habe ich mich entschlossen, mich an Ihre werte Direktion mit der An-
frage zu wenden, ob Herr Ing. Wiesenthal berechtigt war, seine Verfol-
gungen gegen mich und meine Familie , die er bei verschiedenen österr.
Behörden unternommen hat, im Namen des JOINT zu betreiben.

Ich bin überzeugt, dass der JOINT andere Aufgaben als die Er-
stattung von Strafanzeigen gegen jüdische Flüchtlinge hat und niemals
seine Zustimmung dazu geben würde, dass sein Funktionär im Namen dieser
Weltorganisation derartige Handlungen durchführe.

Ich möchte in kurzer Zusammenfassung den Sachverhalt schildern,
wie er sich zugetragen hat:

Ich bin einer der wenigen Naziopfer, die am Leben geblieben sind.
Die Verfolgungsmassnahmen und die erlittenen Misshandlungen im K-Z
haben mich gesundheitlich vollständig ruiniert. Auch meine Gattin ist
schwer krank. Um nicht von Unterstützungen leben zu müssen, habe ich
versucht, mir eine Existenz zu gründen, was mir auch nach vielen An-
strengungen gelungen ist. Ich habe von der Landesregierung in Linz
eine Gewerbeberechtigung erhalten und durch fleissige und ehrliche Arbeit mir mein Brot verdient und daher die Unterstützung des JOINT ver-
zichten konnte. Ich habe von meiner ehrlichen Arbeit für mich, meine
Frau und unsere 2 kleinen Kinder unseren Haushalt gedeckt und von den
Ersparnissen für Wohltätigkeitszwecke nach bester Möglichkeit gespen-
det. Kaum bin ich von den Erlebnissen während der Naziverfolgung ein
wenig zu mir gekommen, hat mich das Unglück " Ing. Wiesenthal " ge-
troffen. Mit Verleumdungen schwersten Kalibers ist er gegen mich im
Namen des JOINT bei den verschiedenen Gerichts-und Verwaltungsbehör-
den aufgetreten und hat solange gegen mich gehetzt, bis ich verhaftet
wurde.

In ihrer Verzweiflung hat meine Gattin, die sich bewusst war,
dass der Aufenthalt für mich im Gefängnis lebensgefährlich ist, sich
an Dr. Winter in Wien mit der Bitte gewendet, meine Enthaftung gegen
eine Haftkaution zu erwirken. Letztgenannter hat sich dazu gegen Be-
zahlung von S 5o.ooo.- als Honorar bereit erklärt. Meine Gattin hat
jüdische Persönlichkeiten in Wien alarmiert, die diesen Betrag zur
Verfügung stellten und ich daraufhin enthaftet wurde.

./.

106

Nach meiner Enthaftung hat mein Rechtsanwalt Einsichtnahme in die Akten verlangt und lege ich eine auszugsweise Abschrift der niederschriftlichen Angaben vor, die zu meiner Verhaftung geführt haben. Ein leitender Beamter des Strafgerichtes in Steyr erklärte meinem Rechtsvertreter, dass es niemals zu meiner Verhaftung gekommen wäre, wenn nicht eine derart massgebende Persönlichkeit, für die Herr Ing. Wiesenthal gehalten wird, diese Verhaftung veranlasst hätte.

Die Gerichtsbehörden fanden keine Bestätigung für die Angaben des Herrn Ing. Wiesenthal gegen mich und ist deshalb eine Verzögerung in der Ausschreibung einer Verhandlung gegen mich eingetreten, obwohl ich diese Verhandlung für meine Rehabilitierung anstrebe.

Was geschehen ist, wird Herr Ing. Wiesenthal niemals wiedergutmachen können. Es steht mir jedoch umstrittig das Recht zu, von demselben zu verlangen, in einer Gegenüberstellung mir ins Gesicht all jene Anschuldigungen zu sagen, die er in seinen Strafanzeigen gegen mich gemacht hat. Um kein Aufsehen zu erregen, erkläre ich mich auch damit einverstanden, dass diese Gegenüberstellung in Ihrem Büro stattfindet.

Ich hoffe, dass Sie dieser Angelegenheit die ihr gebührende Aufmerksamkeit schenken werden und erwarte Ihre baldige Rückäusserung.

Mit vorzüglicher Hochachtung

Cranell

Documents from

Yad Vashem.

Gorodok, Poland. List of persecuted persons murdered. (excerpt)

Lea
Mandel
Grayding, Poland
Page of Testimony
murdered

Yisrael
Mandel
1903
Greiding, Poland
Page of Testimony
murdered

Sara
Mandel
1860
Grodek Jagiellonski, Poland
Page of Testimony
murdered

Wolf
Mandel
Grodek Jagiellonski, Poland
Page of Testimony
murdered

Bronia
Mandel
1914
Grodek Jagiellonski, Poland
Page of Testimony
murdered

Wolf
Mandel
1894
Grodek Jagiellonski, Poland
Page of Testimony
murdered

Tonia
Mandel
1930
Grodek Jagiellonski, Poland
Page of Testimony
murdered

Jaakow
Mandel
1887
Grodek Jagiellonski, Poland
Page of Testimony
murdered

Osiaz Yehoshua
Mandel
1897
Jaworow, Poland
Page of Testimony
murdered

Sara
Mandel
1902
Grodek Jagiellonski, Poland
Page of Testimony
murdered

Chana
Mandel
1907
Grodek Jagiellonski, Poland
Page of Testimony
murdered

Herszl
Mandel
1897
Grodek Jagiellonski, Poland
Page of Testimony
murdered

Tauba
Mandel
1922
Gródek, Poland
Page of Testimony
murdered

Wolf
Mandel
1907
Grodek Jagiellonski, Poland

Page of Testimony
murdered

Mania
Mandel
1900
Grodek Jagiellonski, Poland
Page of Testimony
murdered

Natan
Mandel
1899
Grodek Jagiellonski, Poland
Page of Testimony
murdered

Abraham
Mandel
1872
Grodek Jagiellonski, Poland
Page of Testimony
murdered

Abraham Mandel was born in Grodek Jagiellonski, Poland in 1872. He was a merchant and married to Sara. Prior to WWII he lived in Grodek Jagiellonski, Poland. During the war he was in Grodek Jagiellonski, Poland.

Abraham was murdered in the Shoah.

This information is based on a Page of Testimony submitted by his neighbour, Barukh Salamander

Feiga
Mandel
1917
Grudek Yagyelonski, Poland
Page of Testimony
murdered

Ycchak
Mandel
1921
Grodek Jagiellonski, Poland
Page of Testimony
murdered

Jakob
Mandel
1889
Gródek, Poland
Page of Testimony
murdered

Icchak
Mandel
1922
Grodek Jagiellonski, Poland
Page of Testimony
murdered

Sara
Mandel
1872
Grodek Jagiellonski, Poland
Page of Testimony
murdered

Sara Mandel lived in Grodek Jagiellonski, Poland. During the war she was in Grodek Jagiellonski, Poland.

Sara was murdered in the Shoah.

This information is based on a Page of Testimony submitted by her neighbour, Barukh Salamander

Osias Yehoshua
Mandel
Jaworow, Poland
Page of Testimony
murdered

Gersh
Mandel

Moisey
Mandel

Mosze
Mandel
1902
Grodek Jagiellonski, Poland
Page of Testimony
murdered

Pesach
Mandel
1900
Grodek Jagiellonski, Poland
Page of Testimony
murdered

Rajza
Mandel
1902
Grodek Jagiellonski, Poland
Page of Testimony
murdered

Ana
Mandel
Gródek, Poland
Page of Testimony
murdered

Tonia
Mandel
Gródek, Poland
Page of Testimony
murdered

Tauba Yona
Mandel
1893
Grodek Jagiellonski, Poland
Page of Testimony
murdered

Tzvi
Mandel
Greiding, Poland
Page of Testimony
murdered

Zeev Vilush
Mandel
1913
Greiding, Poland
Page of Testimony
murdered

...

Sara and Abraham Mandel are with high probability the autor's grandparents.

About the other members of the author's family who were murdered in the Shoah exist no documents or records at Yad Vashem.

רשות־זכרון לשואה ולגבורה. ירושלים

דף ־ עד
לרשום חללי השואה והגבורה

ירושלים, רחוב בן־יהודה 12

אבא. מלאני) עד כמה שידוע לך!

מס' השואה № 1887/39

1. שם המשפחה בשפת ארץ המוצא (באותיות לטיניות)	*Mandel* אנ׳ן
2. שם פרטי בשפת ארץ המוצא (באותיות לטיניות)	*Abraham* אברהם
3. שם האב	
4. שם האם	ג׳
5. תאריך הלידה	1872
6. מקום ארץ הלידה (גם באותיות לטיניות)	*Gruder Jag. Pohu.* גרידר
7. מקום המגורים הקבוע (גם באותיות לטיניות)	
8. המקצוע	סוחר
9. הנתינות לפני הכבוש הנאצי	פולני
10. מקומות המגורים במלחמה (גם באותיות לטיניות)	
11. מקום מלות הזמן והנסיבות (מקום גם באותיות לטיניות)	*Gruder* גרידר 161 1942
12. מצב משפחתי	רוק / נשוי / מספר הילדים
13. שם האשה ושם משפחתה לפני הנישאין	גילה 70
	גילו
שם הבעל	

המומם

חוק זכרון השואה והגבורה —
יד ושם
תשי"ג 1953
קובע בסעיף מס' 2
תפקידו של יד־ושם הוא לאסוף אל
המולדת את זכרם של כל אלה מבני
העם היהודי, שנפלו ומסרו את
נפשם, נלחמו ומרדו באויב הנאצי
ובעוזריו, ולהציב שם וזכר להם,
לקהילות, לארגונים ולמוסדות שנחרבו
בגלל השתייכותם לעם הי־
הודי, ולמסורה זו יהא מוסמך —
...(4)להעניק לבני העם היהודי
שהושמדו ונפלו בימי השואה והמרי
אזרחות־"זכרון של מדינת ישראל
לאות היאספם אל עמם.
(ספר החוקים מס' 32,
יום אלול תשי"ג 53.8.28)

14. שמות הילדים עד גיל 18 שנספו (בעל לגיל זה רושמים "דף־עד" פרידו)	הגיל	המקום והזמן שנספו

הערה! את הילדים יש לרשום ב"דף־העד" של אחד ההורים אך לא יוצר מפעם אחת.

אורחות־זכרון הרעיקה

אני 23/160 בן הגר בן (כתובת מלאה) ח תא 115
קרוב/ה מבר/ת צ׳י של אברהם
מצהיר/ה בזה כי העדות שמסרתי כאן על פרטיה היא נכונה ואמתית, לפי מיטב ידיעתי וזכרתי.
אני מבקש/ת להעניק לביל אזרחות־זכרון מטעם מדינת ישראל.
מקום ותאריך חתימה צ׳ תל אביב 24/10
חתימת הפקיד גולדברג אברהם

מספר פו

לידיעת "האגף המרעי" בירושלים. רחוב בן־יהודה 12

הייתי בזמן המלחמה במחנה (הסגר, עבודה, השמדה וכו')		בגיטו
במחתרת	ביערות	וכו'
		ואני מוכן למסור עדות על כך.
תחימת העד	כתובתו	

רשות־זכרון לשואה ולגבורה, ירושלים

דף־עד

לרשום חללי השואה והגבורה

ירושלים, רחוב בן־יהודה 12

אנא, מלא(י) עד כמה שידוע לך!

1. שם המשפחה בשפת ארץ המוצא (באותיות לטיניות)	בעברית אנגל Mendel
2. שם פרטי בשפת ארץ המוצא (באותיות לטיניות)	בעברית שרה Sara
3. שם האב	י.י.
4. שם האם	
5. תאריך הלידה	1872
6. מקום וארץ הלידה (גם באותיות לטיניות)	יגל׳ Gudel Jagel. Polen.
7. מקום המגורים הקבוע (גם באותיות לטיניות)	
8. המקצוע	
9. התנגדות לפני הכבוש הנאצי	
10. מקומות המגורים במלחמה (גם באותיות לטיניות)	
11. מקום המות, הזמן והנסיבות (המקום גם באותיות לטיניות)	יגל׳ Gudel 1942
12. מצב משפחתי	רוק / נשוי / מספר הילדים
13. שם האשה ושם משפחתה לפני הנישואין	גילה

מס׳ האישור 1887/28

חוק זכרון השואה והגבורה —
יד ושם
תשי״ג 1953
קובע בסעיף מס׳ 2

תפקידו של יד ושם הוא לאסוף אל
המולדת את זכרם של כל אלה מבני
העם היהודי, שנפלו ומסרו את
נפשם, נלחמו ומרדו באויב הנאצי
ובעוזריו, ולהציב שם וזכר להם,
לקהילות, לארגונים ולמוסדות שנח־
רבו בגלל השתייכותם לעם הי־
הודי, ולמסרם זו זרע מוסמך —
...(4)להאניק לבני העם היהודי
שהושמדו ונפלו בימי השואה וחברי
אזרחות־זכרון של מדינת ישראל
לאות הראסצף אל עמם.

(ספר החוקים מס׳ 132)
י״ח אלול תשי״ג (28.8.53)

שם הבעל		גיל	המקום והזמן שנספר
		ליד	

14. שמות הילדים עד גיל 18 שנספו (מעל לגיל זה ברשימים "דף־עד" סיוהר)	הגיל	המקום והזמן שנספו

הערה! את הילדים יש לרשום ב"דף־העד" של אחד ההורים אך לא יותר מפעם אחת.

אני שרה אנגל הגר ב (כתובת מלאה) חיפה הן יהודה 115
 קרוב/ה מכ״ר/ה כלה של

מצהיר/ה בזה כי העדות שמסרתי כאן על פרטיה היא נכונה ואמיתית, לפי מיטב ידיעתי וחברתי.

אני מבקש/ת להעניק לנ״ל אזרחות־זכרון מטעם מדינת ישראל.

מקום והאריך _____ חתימה _____
 חתימת המפקיד

אזרחות־זכרון הוענקה
 מספר _____ אל

לידיעת "האנף המדעי" בירושלים, רחוב בן־יהודה 12

הייתי בזמן המלחמה במחנה (הסגר, עבודה, השמדה וכו׳)		בניטו
במחתרת	ביערות	וכו׳
חתימת העד	כתובתו	ואני מוכן למסור עדות על כך.

Yad Vashem Pages of Testimony of Sara and Abraham Mandel.

113

Picture credits

The Mandel family about 1958.